Undefiled
GREAT
NESS

Harnessing the Power of Conflict
to Maximize our Greatest Value

Kevin E. Winters

Undefiled Greatness

Harnessing the Power of Conflict
to Maximize our Greatest Value

By Kevin E. Winters

Published by Kevin E. Winters, 12700 Denny Ct, Upper Marlboro MD
kevinewinterministries@gmail.com

International Standard Book Number:
978-0-9977334-5-7

Printed in the United States of America

Cover design and page layout by Artiest Design and Illustration

Undefiled GREAT NESS

Harnessing the Power of Conflict
to Maximize our Greatest Value

Kevin E. Winters

Preface

Welcome to an exciting journey. I applaud you for taking time to invest in yourself. I also thank you for allowing me to be a part of that process. What I present to you is a beautiful work that I can only describe as a labor of love. Writing it was both a challenge and a pleasure. It was a challenge because it made me look in the mirror and confront my worst enemy—me. It was a pleasure because it helped me maximize greatness in various areas of my life. I am by no means implying that I have reached perfection. Nor am I offering you a cheap quick fix to it. I am, however, saying that I now have knowledge that paves a way towards a better me. I refer to this path as a journey—it was a great one indeed. In fact, I cannot recall a time in my life where a work has produced something so profoundly impacting to my life. I know that it will change yours as well. Though producing this book was a rewarding experience, it was very hard to write. As a writer, the biggest obstacle is conveying an idea that is coherent and digestible to the reader. That is never easy to do when the subject is abstract. Merging a likable topic like greatness with an unpopular one such as conflict was difficult. Just think about it, each one can serve as the subject of its own book. These words even seem to suggest that they are irrelevant to one another. However, I discovered that they are not. In fact, during the writing process, God taught me that one cannot exist without the other. Greatness is attracted to conflict, and conflict is, likewise, drawn to greatness. The dilemma was how to bring these two opposing ideas together to present a practical life-changing product. It was a daunting challenge.

However, God had a fix for the problem. It was called reality. Reality included many different types of conflicts. They all started during the writing of this book. Scattered throughout the chapters are stories regarding a few of them. Through each one God allowed me to intimately realize the principles I present in this book. Oh yes. The Bible declares that the word of the Lord is tested. I am a witness to this truth. God's word to me was definitely tested.

Through each incident, God showed me how to harness the power of the conflicts in my life to teach me how to maximize the greatness within me. As a result, I am a better father, husband, minister, writer, artist, and employee.

During the process, I also discovered that everything

and everyone has the potential to be great. Likewise, I discovered that the glittery luster of greatness is often dimmed. I further learned what steals its shine. Lastly, I discovered what you are going to realize as you read this book; how to remove what hinders your greatness and what it cost to do so.

Let me end with this; as I embarked upon this literary journey, I leaned toward a narrow-minded conclusion. In fact, I did not see the broad application of the principles in is book until I finished writing it. Though this book aims to improve our character, while positively impacting our relationships, my eyes were opened to the reality that the principles that lead to undefiled greatness have many applications. Not only can our relationships benefit from adhering to the precepts God presented me, but even our ideas, inventions, products, skills, work performance, etcetera can profit from His lesson in my life.

As you can see, I learned a lot birthing this wonderful piece of work. Likewise, I am ecstatic about what it is going to do in your life. I am a better me and I am hoping to assist you with becoming a better you!

Contents

Contents

Introduction

Conflict is one of life's most stifling elements. A lot of people believe it is responsible for destroying marriages, friendships, families, careers, nations, and most definitely churches. I, however, would like to suggest that it is not conflict that destroys these precious things in our life, but our lack of knowledge regarding how to respond to it. To most people, conflict is an unwanted intruder. But what if we could harness the power of conflict for the benefit of our growth. Just think about it, conflict is not going anywhere. Even Jesus said, "In this world, you will have trouble" (John 16:33). In other words, Jesus told us to expect, conflict. So, if God is not going to remove conflict, then He must have a purpose for it. After all, Paul tells us that all things are working together for our good (Rom. 8:28). So how does conflict work for our good?

That, my friends, is the question that I hope to answer moving forward. By the time this book ends I intend for you to embrace the value of conflict and use it to harness the power of change. The other thing that you will learn from this book is yet another way that God chooses to speak to us. That's right, the guy who wrote, "God, is that You, Me, or the Devil?" and "You Can hear the Voice of God Clearly" is going to show you a remarkable truth about the voice of God in conflict.

One of the things I often do is use the voice of God in counseling. That being the case, I have some experience in regard to the types of conflicts in the lives of people, churches, communities, and workplaces. I have at some point counseled persons from one of these groups. That means that I often get to help people understand what God is saying to them through the conflict in their lives. Likewise, I intend to do the same for you.

To accomplish this task, I am going to unveil the truth that is tucked away in a familiar biblical story. It is the story of a man who dared to believe that his life could be different. He believed that he could obtain his dream. That dream was to experience restoration and wholeness. In his life restoration represented something God wanted for him. For you, restoration may be the next big career move, or a healed marriage, or a healed friendship, or the next level of ministry. Restoration can represent any number of things. For Naaman restoration meant healing.

I want you to ask yourself what it is in your life that represents the dream God has for you? That is an important question to answer as we move forward. It's important because we are going to look at how the conflicts in Naaman's life contributed to that goal. We are also going to look at how an inappropriate response to conflict can undermine it.

Ultimately, I am going to teach you how to use the conflicts in your life to your advantage!

Naaman's Story

Since the main idea of this book centers on the life of Naaman, I provided the text for you. Please read it and familiarize yourself with the story. I am primarily providing the text for those readers who may not know anything about Naaman's story.

2 Kings 5:1-14
New King James Version (NKJV)
Naaman Is Healed

Now Naaman, commander of the army of the king of Syria, was a great and honorable man in the eyes of his master, because by him the LORD had given victory to Syria. He was also a mighty man of valor, but a leper. ² And the Syrians had gone out on raids, and had brought back captive a young girl from the land of Israel. She waited on Naaman's wife. ³ Then she said to her mistress, "If only my master were with the prophet who is in Samaria! For he would heal him of his leprosy." *4* And Naaman went in and told his master, saying, "Thus and thus said the girl who is from the land of Israel."

5 Then the king of Syria said, "Go now, and I will send a letter to the king of Israel."

So he departed and took with him ten talents of silver, six thousand shekels of gold, and ten changes of clothing. *6* Then he brought the letter to the king of Israel, which said,

Now be advised, when this letter comes to you, that I have sent Naaman my servant to you, that you may heal him of his leprosy.

7 And it happened, when the king of Israel read the letter, that he tore his clothes and said, "Am I God, to kill and make alive, that this man sends a man to me to heal him of his leprosy? Therefore please consider, and see how he seeks a quarrel with me."

8 So it was, when Elisha the man of God heard that the king of Israel had torn his clothes, that he sent to the king, saying, "Why have you torn your clothes? Please let him come to me, and he shall know that there is a prophet in Israel."

⁹ Then Naaman went with his horses and chariot, and he stood at the door of Elisha's house. ¹⁰ And Elisha sent a messenger to him, saying, "Go and wash in the Jordan seven times, and your flesh shall be restored to you, and you shall be clean." ¹¹ But Naaman became furious, and went away and said, "Indeed, I said to myself, 'He will surely come out to me, and stand and call on the name of the LORD his God, and wave his hand over the place, and heal the leprosy.' ¹² Are not the Abanah [a] and the Pharpar, the rivers of Damascus, better than all the waters of Israel? Could I not wash in them and be clean?" So he turned and went away in a rage. ¹³ And his servants came near and spoke to him, and said, "My father, if the prophet had told you to do something great, would you not have done it? How much more then, when he says to you, 'Wash, and be clean'?" ¹⁴ So he went down and dipped seven times in the Jordan, according to the saying of the man of God; and his flesh was restored like the flesh of a little child, and he was clean.

¹⁵ And he returned to the man of God, he and all his aides, and came and stood before him; and he said, "Indeed, now I know that there is no God in all the earth, except in Israel; now, therefore, please take a gift from your servant."

¹⁶ But he said, "As the LORD lives, before whom I stand, I will receive nothing." And he urged him to take it, but he refused.

17 So Naaman said, "Then, if not, please let your servant be given two mule-loads of earth; for your servant will no longer offer either burnt offering or sacrifice to other gods, but to the LORD. 18 Yet in this thing may the LORD pardon your servant: when my master goes into the temple of Rimmon to worship there, and he leans on my hand, and I bow down in the temple of Rimmon—when I bow down in the temple of Rimmon, may the LORD please pardon your servant in this thing."

19 Then he said to him, "Go in peace." So he departed from him a short distance.

Chapter 1

As a Man Thinks

One of the most quoted verses in the Bible is Proverbs 23:7. It reads, "As a man thinks in his heart so is he." One day, as I was driving to work this verse became the subject of my conversation with God. During the conversation, He said a profound thing about this verse. He said, "I want to straighten something out!" It was a shocking statement because I thought I already understood this verse. After all, this is a common verse that a believer might hear in a sermon several times in a year. When stated, it is usually a declaration warning us against becoming what we think. Lately, it has even been used to justify the idea of the imagination as a literal place where we sin. So, God's statement was a bit captivating for me because it implied that we have been interpreting this verse wrong.

By making such a statement, God aroused my curiosity, and I could not help but give Him my full attention. What

He said next was so life changing for me that I have not been the same since. He said, "Your imagination is a reflection of the person in your heart, and your thoughts are a reflection of your reality." I will never forget that. Then He went on to further explain to me how it all works.

If you, like myself, have heard that we become what we think then this is quite the departure from that idea. It is a departure primarily because God seems to suggest that the opposite is true. He is not saying that we are going to become what we think, but that we are what we think. Some of you may be a bit put off by that idea. Nonetheless, offensive or not, it is true. Your thought life reveals who you are. Stay with me. Keep reading. This is a good thing, I promise! Understanding this truth is the basis for seeing growth and change in your life. I can guarantee you this, embracing this reality will allow you to see a difference in yourself. I have met plenty of stagnant Christians over the years—some of them complaining about not growing in Christ in over 20 years! Might this truth be the missing key to their growth? As I said earlier, understanding this truth has forever changed my life. Likewise, if you keep reading it is going to change yours as well.

The Inner-Outer Conflict

Let me see if I can put you at ease a little and clarify what God means by the definition He provided. It is not foreign to anyone reading this book that sometimes we present the world with our representative. Our representative is the version of ourselves that we deem acceptable for any given situation. For instance, sometimes people are required to accompany clients to dinner and other social-work-related events. This often requires a level of decorum on the part of the service provider that includes making a lasting impression on the client. Doing so may require laughing at their jokes, complimenting them on various things, and being pleasant company. This behavior, however, can be a façade. I have been in these types of situations. I was laughing on the outside, while thinking to myself, "I can't wait for this to be over. I swear if I never see this person again in my lifetime, I will not be angry." So, the behavior I displayed outwardly was not a reflection of the truth reflected in my thoughts.

I'll give you another example. Due to the level of revelation that I get from God, I am often complimented regarding my gifting. One of the compliments I seem to get a lot is about how humble I am in light of my gift. The funny thing is, most people have no idea that I have battled prideful thoughts. They were completely oblivious to my struggle because I learned how to hide it. Also, my pastor is a great role model of genuine humility. I knew how it looked and I knew how to get into character. I knew all the right things to say, "Oh, thank you, it's not about me, it's about God" or "Give God the glory" or "I'm nothing, you can do it too." I had all the church jargon down tight; still, inwardly I was another person. I was humble on the outside and prideful on the inside. Be that as it may, because we live in a tactile reality people only saw the physical part of me. That is the problem that most of us have. We can contribute our propensity to hide who we truly are to many factors. We will look at some of these factors later in the book.

I will never forget listening to a news report regarding the capture of a serial killer. What made it such a compelling story was the fact that the serial killer was also a well-regarded deacon in his church. It was so shocking to think that there was a very deviant-minded person in the church—one who had so viciously preyed on women. If my memory serves me correctly, not only did he brutally kill multiple women, he also taunted the police about not solving the murders. This man is a classic example of a person that displays one thing on the outside while struggling with another reality in his heart.

Jesus said in Matthew 15:19, that murder, adultery, sexual immorality, theft, false testimony, and slander come out of the heart. All this means that it is possible to have these things hiding in our hearts, though we may never physically do them.

Here is something else to consider as we look at the inner-outer conflict principle. Genesis 6:5 says, "Then the LORD saw that the wickedness of man was great in the earth, and that every intent of the thoughts of his heart was only evil continually." Most of us believe that God destroyed the world the first time because of mankind's evil actions. Though the verse mentions the wickedness of humanity, it clarifies the source of the wickedness. It says that God saw the "intent of the thoughts" or the imaginations of mankind. God saw that human beings only imagined evil things. He saw the rotten inner person.

Cain is a perfect example. He did something righteous in Genesis 4:2. He offered something to God. Yet, God's refusal of his gift revealed that he had something deviant on the inside. God said, "Cain, if you do well, will you not be received. But be careful, sin lies at the door..." In other words, while what you display outwardly is good, something sinister is hiding in your heart. Not long after his encounter with God, the sin that laid at the door made itself at home in Cain's heart. Then he rose up and killed his brother.

Another Great Biblical Example

You may be wondering if there are other biblical examples of this idea. Sure there is, and we can see them in some very familiar passages of scripture.

One such example is presented in the story of Samuel anointing David to be Israel's new king. In 1 Samuel 16:1-13 we read of the prophet Samuel coming to the house of a man named Jesse. It was his divine assignment to anoint the next king since God had spiritually dethroned King Saul. I use the term *spiritually* because God removed His Spirit from Saul, though He allowed him to continue to serve as king. In fact, He replaced the anointing of the Holy Spirit with an evil spirit (See verses 16:14). That shows us that Samuel was spiritually enthroning David.

When we pick up the story in 1 Samuel 16:4-13, Samuel is attempting to fulfill his assignment. After entering the house of Jesse, he immediately sets his eyes on Eliab the oldest son. In an instant, he assumes that he is God's choice for king. After all, according to Samuel, he was a robust good-looking fellow (verse 6,7). This conclusion was not farfetched. Even the Bible describes King Saul this way. Likewise, God Himself had chosen him to be the first king. That being the case, the idea of God considering a choice that had the appearance of a king was not a foreign concept. So, Samuel went on down the line making assumptions based on the appearance of these guys. It would not be long before God said to Him, "God does not see as man sees. Man looks at the outward appearance, but God looks at the heart." (1 Sam. 16:7)

This statement became an instant classic that would reverberate throughout many pulpits in the world. It also communicates that God sees things about people that no human can see. This difference in viewpoint becomes evident as Samuel exhausts his search for a king in the house. Finally, he had to consider God's nontraditional approach. With this conclusion in mind, he asks Jesse if all of his sons were present. Jesse responds by informing Samuel that he has one more son that is out tending the sheep. Therefore, Samuel has Jesse send for the last son. His name is David.

When David comes into the house the Lord says to Samuel, "This is the one!" I can only imagine the look on the prophet's face as he finds himself face to face with a cute little teenager; A dirty and smelly teenager who tends sheep. There was nothing honorable or kingly about David's appearance. In those days the king went out to battle with the soldiers. In fact, the king led the charge. I can again imagine Samuel's face as he tries to picture this cute little boy leading the armies of the great God of Israel. I can imagine him thinking to himself, "Lord, shouldn't a king look big and strong like those guys? How is this little guy going to strike fear into the heart of our enemies?"

It would not be long before the king that God saw in David's heart revealed himself. Later on, in chapter 16, these same brothers find themselves in a dilemma. They are a part of the Israeli military and are now facing the prospect of fighting a 9 foot 6 inch man. When we catch up to them in the story, they are hiding with the army in a ditch.

The story gets even better when Jesse sends David to the battlefield to serve his brothers. Just picture him coming to the battle and seeing an empty battlefield. I'm sure he wondered, "Hey, where is everybody?" Then he looked down and there sat the entire army hiding in a ditch from one man. Guess who was there hiding among them. If you guessed the brothers, you are absolutely right! I know that you are thinking, "Wait a minute! These are the same men that Samuel assumed were fit to be king of Israel.

Wait! There is more. The story takes an exciting turn when the giant of a man, named Goliath, challenges the army of Israel and insults the name of God. This act of disrespect catches the ear of David and before you know it he was ready to go to war.

Are you seeing what God showed me yet? You see, God saw the king in David's heart. Even though he was frail, God saw the bravery and sense of commitment concealed by the small frame of a teenager. He also saw the coward that was living in the heart of David's brothers; the cowardice hidden behind strapping shoulders and deep voices.

Who they truly were inside was different from who they were outside. Likewise, their thoughts revealed what was in their heart. Their action, hiding, was a clear indication of the fearful thoughts that filled their mind. We do not know what they said to themselves, but their actions tell us that whatever they said about the issue was not consistent with the behavior of brave men. Jesus said, out of the abundance of the heart the mouth speaks (See Luke 6:45). This statement shows us that what they said was a revelation of the thoughts of their heart. The same can be said for David. In fact, he explicitly shows us his thought process. We see his rationale in his explanation to King Saul regarding the source of his confidence in the belief that he can defeat Goliath, the Philistine champion.

Naaman

Our last example is the main character of our discussion, Naaman. I will not go into detail about his inner-outer conflict now, but we will look at his story to understand how God exposes us to what is hiding in our heart. In my opinion, he is the epitome of the idea of inner-outer conflict. His story is found in 2 Kings 5:1-14. It teaches us that sometimes the things that hide in our heart have everything to do with our inability to receive God's best for our lives. As we examine his story, you will undoubtedly see that God had agreed to bless him and change his circumstances. However, something threatened his ability to receive his miracle. Likewise, I believe that something is threatening the reception of your miracle too.

How to Use This Book

Our the end of each chapter are reflection activity questions. Each is designed to help you review and recall information from the chapters. Please complete them all.

Also, each activity section requires you to write. You may do so on a blank sheet of paper, or you may order the *Undefiled Greatness Journaling Workbook.*

Reflection Activity:

- Take a moment to consider the inner-outer principle. In what way is this principle visible in your life?

- Ask yourself the question, "What is holding up God's miracle in my life?" If you believe that you know the answer to the question, write it in the space provided or in a journal. After reading through the book your answer may change. It may even grow!

- If you cannot answer the question, that's ok. Keep reading. This book is designed to help you discover the answer and the solution to the problem.

- Read through the book, completing all of the "Reflection Activities." Upon completion, return to this section to update your answer and record the solution to the problem.

As a Man Thinks

The Problem: _____

_____
_____
_____
_____
_____
_____
_____
_____
_____
_____

The Solution: _____

_____
_____
_____
_____
_____
_____
_____
_____
_____
_____
_____

Chapter 2

When Greatness is Blemished

Can I tell you that you are great? You may not realize it now, but the Bible calls every believer God's handiwork (See Eph. 2:10). You are a work in progress and every day is God's tool to craft in you the vision He has planned for your life. You should know, however, that greatness can be blemished. Not only can your personal greatness be blemished, but anything great can be blemished. The greatness of your marriage, career, family relationships, church and much more, can all be blemished.

We learn about blemished greatness reading about Naaman in 2 Kings 5. The first part of the story regarding his life is fantastic. He had career status. He had honor bestowed on him by the king. Lastly, he was revered in war. Naaman was a great man indeed. The only problem was that he was a leper, according to 1 Kings 5:1. He had a disease that was just as visible to the outer world as his accomplishments.

Sure, they saw the battle scars that proved to be an indicator of his unmatched warrior status. Sure, they saw the multitudes of soldiers that confidently placed their lives in his hands and came home safely to their families. Sure, they saw the way the king doted over this mere human. Nonetheless, they also saw his issue.

Some of you may not understand the complexity of leprosy. Leprosy is a skin disease in which the affected area becomes discolored and rots over time. The condition can be so extreme that the affected area dies entirely and falls from the body. This means that Naaman was in a position to lose something. It may appear to you by my description of leprosy that Naaman was at risk of losing a physical part of himself. However, I would like to suggest that his potential lost was far more significant. He was at risk of losing his dignity. He was at risk of losing his great name and the respect of all who would come to admire him. What is a soldier without an arm? Or what good is a mighty man without his legs? What use is a sword to a man that has lost his hand? Folks, Naaman was at risk of losing what he had worked so hard to achieve. He was at risk of losing his greatness!

In fact, I would also like to suggest that it had already started happening. In reading this text, I was amazed by Naaman's resume. I was not only amazed at how great he was on paper, but by how blemished he was by his issue. I mean, the writer spent all that time listing his great achievements only to blemish it with, "...but, Naaman was a leper." The writer put his "but" in Naaman's business, and now our thinking regarding him shifts to something negative.

You see, "but" is a conjunction used to bring two sentences or phrases together. It is also used to make comparisons. It also has the unique power of diminishing the power of the first phrase or sentence. For instance, I could say Naaman was great even though he had leprosy. Or, I could say, "Naaman was great, and he had leprosy." Neither of these two sentences diminishes Naaman's accomplishments. Howbeit, when I use the term "but" I am immediately casting a shadow over all that Naaman achieved to inform you that there is a more significant issue; one that is greater than his life accomplishments.

Having blemished greatness may seem unique to Naaman. However, you too have areas in your life where a visible issue overshadows your greatness. If we put Naaman's life into today's context, it could easily read, "The pastor was a great man who built many churches, birthed many world-changing ministers, but he cheated on his wife." Or, it could have read, "Naaman was a great businessman who changed the landscape of his community and impacted the lives of the youth, but he was a gambler." Likewise, it could have read, "Naaman was a great husband who raised great children, but he had an anger problem." Or, "Naaman was a great speaker, but he was shy." Put your name in for Naaman's, and I'm sure you will see how easy it is for someone to put his or her "but" in your business. What this means is that all of us can have our greatness overshadowed by our issues.

Speaking for myself, I can attest to the reality of this truth. I can remember growing up as a kid who dared to dream, and I dreamed a lot! I always had an idea in my head. At one point I was a fashion designer. At another time I was a rapper. Then I was an artist. I have always been the guy that told everyone I was going to do this and that. Despite how many times I imagined achieving my dreams, I failed every time. I did not fail because things did not work out. I failed because I was afraid to try and too undisciplined to finish what I started.

As you might imagine, people were a little tired of hearing about my plans. After a while, it was as if I were the boy who cried wolf.

Now, anyone who knew me back then would tell you that I was talented. I have been an artist since I was five years old. I am also gifted in how I use words and images to communicate. My ability to creatively use words and pictures made me a great rapper and poet. I had access to my greatness. Likewise, everyone admired what I could do. Be that as it may, I was undisciplined and fearful. I had a blemish on my greatness. I am willing to bet that you do too.

Nevertheless, blemish or no blemish, you should know that you are great. Likewise, it is that greatness that I intend to help you unveil.

Reflection Activity:

- Take a moment to think about the great things in your life. Remember, that can include talents, skills, roles (parental, supervisor, etc.), your marriage, your church, your congregation, and even your relationship with other races and ethnic groups. Anything area of your life can be great. Likewise, its greatness can be blemished.

- Next, take time to consider what it is that blemishes your greatness. Ask yourself the question, "What is keeping me, and things connected to me from maximizing God's greatness in my life?"

Chapter 3

It's Not Just Affecting You

I am always amazed at the number of people who dare to believe that their problems are theirs alone. They say such things as, "I ain't hurting nobody with my..." Consequently, people affected by their actions also say, "You ain't hurting nobody but yourself." This type of logic is part of our human security system. It is what we tell ourselves to protect ourselves from being hurt. Nevertheless, the truth is our issues, though ours, affects everyone around us.

God taught me this truth as I was studying Naaman's life. It is my routine to study the scriptures when preparing messages. It is usually a selected passage because I was trained to use the expository preaching method. That means that I look to expose the central truth in the selected passage. Doing so requires a lot of study and observation. However, I have also spent many years immersing myself in various Christian cultures and practices. Immersing myself in various church cultures means that I was exposed to different methods of investigating scripture. One method I learned was revelatory study. Revelatory study involves allowing the Holy Spirit to unveil hidden realities in the scriptures. So, after I read, study, and observe the text, gleaning from it bits and pieces of insight, I go to God. I go to Him to discuss the insights I saw in the text. I also depend on Him to interpret those insights. As I am seeking to allow Him to open the floodgates of revelation: I say to Him, "Okay God, I have studied this passage and found what I can by my effort. Now, show me what I don't see." Then I close the Bible. With the passage in mind, I then listen for His voice. That is when the magic happens. All of a sudden God makes the things I studied come to life. He also adds to them His ideas and shows me things I could not have seen by merely examining the passage.

As I was studying Naaman's life, He showed me something that I had never seen before. Read the passage below:

> *And the Syrians had gone out on raids, and had brought back captive a young girl from the land of Israel. She waited on Naaman's wife.* [3] *Then she said to her mistress, "If only my master were with the prophet who is in Samaria! For he would heal him of his leprosy."* [4] *And Naaman went in and told his master, saying, "Thus and thus said the girl who is from the land of Israel."* [5] *Then the king of Syria said, "Go now, and I will send a letter to the king of Israel." So he departed and took*

with him ten talents of silver, six thousand shekels of gold, and ten changes of clothing. ⁶ Then he brought the letter to the king of Israel, which said, Now be advised, when this letter comes to you, that I have sent Naaman my servant to you, that you may heal him of his leprosy. ⁷ And it happened, when the king of Israel read the letter, that he tore his clothes and said, "Am I God, to kill and make alive, that this man sends a man to me to heal him of his leprosy? Therefore please consider, and see how he seeks a quarrel with me." ⁸ So it was, when Elisha the man of God heard that the king of Israel had torn his clothes, that he sent to the king, saying, "Why have you torn your clothes? Please let him come to me, and he shall know that there is a prophet in Israel." (2 Kings 5:1-8 NKJV)

As you read the passage, did you notice the broad reach of Naaman's problem? In verse 1, it was a personal issue. In verses 2-3 Naaman's wife and her servant were discussing his issue. Reading about the discussion in his house shows us that his personal issue was also a domestic issue. All of this led to verse 5 when the king of Syria came into the picture. Then the king of Syria involved the king of Israel in Naaman's problem. So, get the Picture; Naaman's issues became a domestic issue, then a national issue, finally, an international issue.

Looking at the broad scope of impact regarding Naaman's issue means that we cannot make assumptions. We cannot assume we alone are affected by our gambling habit. Neither can we assume that our drug addiction does not affect our loved ones and even our communities. We also cannot assume that behavior such as procrastination does not financially affect our family. Finally, we cannot pretend that our issues, as men and women of God, whether Apostles, Prophets, Evangelists, Pastors, or Teachers, do not affect the congregation to whom we minister. Wherever you serve in society, know that your issue has legs and travels abroad impacting the lives of others. Sometimes that impact is felt as far away from you as one can go. Oh, how I long for the day when God's voice penetrates the heart of humanity and illuminates his heart so that he realizes that what he does indeed matter.

Less my rhetoric makes you feel hopeless, let me spread a little sunlight on this section. I want you to know that even though Naaman's personal issue became an international issue, it didn't stop there. Verse 8 says that Elisha, the man of God heard it. Elisha hearing about Naaman's problem is good news. It is good news because someone heard about the issue that had the power and courage to change it. Also, I want you to know that God will always ensure that He places someone in your path that will partner with you to change your circumstances.

While it is an excellent thing that Naaman's issue found its way to a man connected to God. It is an even higher honor that Naaman's issue (that was personal in verse 1) is now God's issue in verse 8. God involved Himself in

Naaman's crisis. God is also involved in yours. May I encourage you that your problem is never your problem. It is everyone's problem; your family; your community; your government; your international government; the churches, and most importantly God's.

There is an old proverb that says, "It takes a village to raise a child." Naaman's life is the very depiction of the power of unity and community. Everyone agreed that Naaman had a problem. Likewise, everyone decided to help Naaman resolve it. May we all wake up to the power of community and work as a team to solve the challenges in our homes, churches, and nations.

As an American, I readily see this truth at work. My country is thought to be the greatest country on the face of the earth. It is powerful beyond imagination, wealthy to no end, and full of endless possibilities for immigrants to rise to greatness. It is indeed a great nation. However, we suffer from racial despair, misogyny, economic selfishness, and hardness of heart towards the less fortunate. Our issues, like Naaman's, threaten our greatness and possibly the stability of the world.

It is the year 2016, and I prophesied in early 2015 that God was going to stir up conflict in our nation. He has definitely done so. Watching Him pull the covers back has been an amazing experience. As He did this great country suddenly saw issues arise that tore at its very fabric. Personally, I was shocked at how our issues impacted the lives of neighboring countries. I was oblivious to how government and money worked. The word economy was just a fancy word in a conversation among crazed political fans. Now I know what these concepts are and how impacting they are to our lives.

What I want you to think about regardless of your country or national affiliation is how you contribute to the greatness or lack thereof, of your nation. You see, just like Naaman, the national and international issues are a symptom of issues in our home and heart. What role are you going to play in what happens on the international stage? Is there an issue in your life that you assume affects you only? Is it your issue that is overshadowing your greatness? That is a personal question, a national question, an international question, and a question for the religious community as well.

I want to end this chapter asking that question again. What is overshadowing your greatness? How is that something affecting the lives of those around you and those abroad?

Reflection Activity:

- Take a moment to think about how your issue has affected the lives of those around you. As you do, consider how it affected your life, those close to you, your community, and your world.

- Make a list of things and people affected by your issues. This may be hard for some people to do but do it anyway. It is very important to identify your issues. It is equally important that you recognized the broad impact it has on the lives of those around you. As you make your list do not allow guilt to consume you. By the end of this book, understanding this principle will aid you in healing what has hurt others.

Chapter 4

The Revelation in Tension

I n the last chapter, we looked at how much impact Naaman's personal problem had on the world. Now I want to look at how God uses our outer issue to show us deeper issues of the heart. One thing that is admirable about Naaman is the tremendous amount of support he was able to garner. I also admire the fact that he did not sit around complaining about the circumstances in his life. He took action to resolve the problem.

I am an avid watcher of shows like "Intervention" and "Lockup." These types of stories captivate me for some reason. Watching these shows often reminds me that people must have a desire for change before change can happen. Naaman wanted a change in his life. It was that desire that ultimately drove him to a God encounter.

Passion and Opportunity

I think that sometimes we forget how powerful passion is in our lives. Jesus said in Matthew 5:6, "Blessed are those that hunger and thirst, for they shall be filled." That is a statement about passion. There is something compelling about a strong desire. Something that I know most people misunderstand is that no one lives without passion. It is our passions that give life to anything that we touch. Unfortunately, some people do not realize that passion needs direction and focus.

Some would say addicts, strippers, and criminals lack passion when comparing such persons to athletes, college students, and career professionals. I, however, disagree. I believe that no one lives without passion. A misguided focus is the problem not a lack of passion. While the college student is passionate about learning; the drug addict is passionate about the high. The pursuits of both are rooted in passion. Yet their passions are directed towards different goals.

When discussing the subject of passion, the same can be said about Naaman. It is clear that he was passionate about his career. He was also passionate about his healing. I think we can all agree that his passion for these things was noble. Nonetheless, what happens when your passion becomes someone else's pain? What happens when you are hurting so bad that when you see an opportunity for help, you cause unintentional pain? Sometimes it is not people that get hurt, but other things.

For example, after nine months of pregnancy, a woman

sees the day of delivery as her opportunity for relief. The fact that it comes with a cost does not mean a thing to her. When those labor pains hit, she does not care if she has insurance or not. She does not care that her decision and passion to push will result in possible financial calamity. She only cares about getting her issue resolved. That being the case, her finances may take a hit because of her passion to be delivered.

Some of you reading this don't know about this kind of pain. There is a level a pain one can experience that will make you knock your mama over, ruin your credit, jack up your relationships, and it won't be personal. It's just the result of passion meeting opportunity.

This also happened to Naaman. He had a problem that he was passionately trying to resolve. The problem was that in his passionate pursuit he put lives at risk. The text shows us that his personal issue grew from personal to domestic to national. This, however, was not the problem, per se. The problem came to light when the national issue became an international issue. It occurred when the king of Syria sent his nation's personal problem to be resolved by the king of Israel.

Notice what the king of Israel said in verse 7, "Am I God, to kill and make alive, that this man sends a man to me to heal him of his leprosy? Therefore, please consider, and see how he seeks a quarrel with me." Ok, Houston, we have a problem! Naaman's problem is now Israel's responsibility.

I remember something that happened when my mother-in-law died. After her death, she left behind a small debt. In an effort to notify her creditors of her passing we called each one to relay to them that she was deceased. After hanging up the phone, we were sure that everything was resolved. That was until we got a bill in the mail attempting to assign the debt to us. Understanding what I do now, I know that the passion driving them had nothing to do with us. They saw an opportunity to resolve their problem and pursued it. Somehow, they wanted her problem to become our responsibility.

If you have ever had to be responsible for someone else's problem I want to encourage you. Please know that passion is not personal. The addict is passionate about the high, but the hurt they cause you is not meant to be personal. There is something to be satisfied, and unfortunately, it causes personal hurt. The same truth applies to the gambler, the workaholic mom or dad, etc. Passion is not personal though it often affects us on a personal level.

When my wife returned to work, she hit the ground running. She had sat on her dream for 12 long years. Being back in the workforce was exciting for her, and all she saw going forward was freedom. On one occasion she made plans to attend a conference out of state. The conference was a training program that would better position her to fulfill her dream. With excitement in her heart she booked her flight for 6:00 a.m. central time. That meant that I had to get up at 3:50 a.m. to be out of the house by 4:10 a.m. to get her to the airport, which was 25 miles away. After dropping her off at the airport, I would have to rush home to get our four kids ready for school. Also, her great-aunt had come to stay with us a few months earlier. So, I had to get her ready for her elderly daycare as well. There was a lot to do.

A couple of days prior to her departure she told me that she was taking an Uber to the airport. With a guilty conscience, I said, "No problem." Then the day before her flight she asked if I would take her to the airport. I was immediately upset. I was upset because I knew that taking her to the airport meant I would be racing against the clock to get home. However, I did not want my wife in the car with a stranger at 4 o'clock in the morning, so I complied with her request.

At the time, I felt so annoyed that she did not plan it out better. I know I sound like a jerk, but that is how I felt. On the way home from the airport, I complained to God about the situation. Then He said to me, "Kevin, passion is not personal!" All of a sudden, I reflected on the truth in this section of the book. It was true. My wife was not trying to annoy me or hurt me in any way. She was not trying to make my morning hard. She was trying to reach a dream that had been on hold for 12 years. She was trying to make good use of her two advanced degrees and her love for empowering children. She was in hot pursuit of her dream. Likewise, I mistook her passion as a personal attack. Many of you have done the same. You have taken passion personally.

Naaman was passionate too. He was so passionate that his passion created problems for the entire nation. In fact, it created problems for both nations. If anything went wrong, the two would have gone to war and lives would have been lost because of Naaman's passion. That being said, his actions were not personal. They were not the result of an intentional decision to cause harm. They were the result of his passion. Don't allow your heart to take issue with hurting people who offended you on their way to resolving their issue, even those who take the wrong approach to doing so.

The Prophetic Act

As we look at this story closely, we see the most incredible prophetic act take shape in the passage. The term "prophetic" refers to the forecasting of an idea in the text. And hidden in the text's problem is a revelation. Most people do not realize that prophecy loves problems. Show me a problem, and I'll show you a prophecy opening up in the midst of it. The Bible says an encounter with prophecy will expose the secrets of the heart (See 1 Cor. 14:25).

Something is about to be exposed and it happens in verse 7. The Bible says that the king tore his robe after Naaman's passion for resolving his problem landed on his doorstep. The act of tearing the robe is yet another layer of conflict in this story. Until now, I have purposely held back showing you all of the conflicts in the story. That being the case, I want you to know that this story is riddled with conflict.

First, there was a conflict in the reading of Naaman's resume, "Naaman was a great a mighty man, and honorable man, but he was a leper." There was conflict in Naaman's home. His wife and his servant were talking about his issue. There was a conflict between the kings now that the king of Syria was imposing on the king of Israel. There are even more conflicts in the text that we will explore moving forward. The one that sets the tone for God's restoration, however, happened as the king tore his robe. Surprisingly, there is a revelation in this action.

In biblical times, the tearing of the robe was a custom. People often reacted this way to a problem. In fact, we see it in several other places in scripture. (Gen. 37:34, Judges 11:34-35, 2 Sam. 1:11-12, 13:30-31, 2 Kings 2:11-12, Job 1:20, Acts 14:14). It was an outward action that conveyed to onlookers the inner concern of the one who tore the robe. Likewise, when the king tore his robe, he expressed the issues of his heart. Interesting, Naaman's issue became the conduit to the issue that arose in the king's heart. In addition, the king's issue was veiled behind his outer garment.

Tension is the Catalyst to Revelation

Now, what makes the king's act of tearing his robe prophetic? To unpack the revelation in this part of the story I need to point out a few things. First, to tear the robe the king had to use opposing force to create tension on the parts of the garment held together by a common thread. This example teaches us something about tension. It communicates to us that we are subject to tearing whenever we experience tension in our life. It can be a tear in our relationships with our friends, wives, co-workers, a tear in our careers, a tear in our congregation, and even a tear within us. It further communicates to us that tension is often the door to the hidden places within us. Like the king, we may find that tension causes us to open up about hidden things in our heart. Finally, it teaches us that all tension originates from what I call the commonplace.

The Commonplace Principle

The commonplace is the point of origin for the tension. It may be a shared goal or idea. In the story it is the thread that held the king's garment together. In our lives, we may have areas where there is tension that has two or more forces pulling in opposite directions and one place that each side holds in common. All tension originates from a "commonplace." For instance, a common issue in marriage revolves around sex — how often, how much? It never fails that there is one person who wants sex more than the other. The commonplace is sex. Generally, both persons want it. However, they often stand on opposite ends of that commonplace. Standing on opposite ends of this issue often creates much friction. Friction usually starts with the commonplace. The commonplace in a situation can be a shared desire to hang out, a shared desire to get married, a shared desire to get to work, a shared desire to buy a car, etc. Anything can be a commonplace from which tension arises. Likewise, the driving force will be the passionate pursuit of the goal from differing points of view.

Putting it All Together

Now, let's put it all together. We can see that the tearing of the king's robe has a significance to the story. Again, the tearing leads to the exposure of something deeper. That tear is the result of a shared desire. This all reveals to us that the tension on the outside was a gateway to the issue on the inside.

Believe it or not, this small gesture by the king is actually forecasting what is about to happen in the interaction between Naaman and Elisha. The opposing force between them; the one that originated from the desire to see Naaman healed is about to create a tear. And that tear is about to expose something deeper than leprosy!

In the next chapter I will go into deeper explanation of my last statement. We will answer the question, "What's behind that tear?"

Reflection Activity:

- What are you passionate about? Has that passion caused problems in your life?

- Now that you understand that passion is not personal consider forgiving those who may have innocently hurt you in the pursuit of their passion; even those who were pursuing the wrong kinds of things.

- Consider how your passion contributes to the tension in your life. What is the commonplace from which the tension originates?

Chapter 5

What is Behind that Tear

The most intriguing thing about 2 Kings chapter 5 is the hidden idea in the passage. Most people who read or preach this passage build their sermons and teachings on the most obvious idea in the text—Naaman's pride and his healing. There is, however, a theme even more critical to the story than either of the prior mentioned lessons. That theme is one of seeing what is in the heart.

Can I ask you a question? What is in your heart? Jeremiah, the prophet, declared in the 17th chapter and 9th verse of his book, that the heart is desperately wicked. He then goes on to ask the question, "Who can know what is in it?" What the prophet is declaring is the truth that sometimes we do things without consciously being aware of the reason. Have you ever considered why you drink, or sabotage budding relationships, or go into fits of anger, or follow destructive people, or procrastinate? Most of us never consider why we behave a certain way. In fact, we have become accustomed to saying to ourselves, "Oh, that's just the way I am." When we do this, we unwittingly give our heart permission to behave in inappropriate ways. Consequently, and unfortunately, it often comes back to haunt us.

As I was writing the first draft of this book, I had an experience that will forever change who I am. It all started with an argument with my wife but led to me eventually going through a healing process. It had been a good day. I was enjoying my wife of 14 years, who had just gone back to work part-time. She did so after sacrificing 12 years of her career to raise our four children. As we sat having a pleasant discussion, I suddenly took a stern position regarding her employment. At the time, she had just accepted a part-time consulting job that promised flexible hours. However, it did not deliver on its promise. That meant that our schedules were thrown into sudden chaos. On top of that, she was already tutoring, plus she had just taken on another small job. To top it off, she had a home business that was tedious. As you can see, I had an active stay-at-home wife. I never worried about her sitting around eating bonbons and being lazy. It is just not in her genetic structure to do nothing. With all of this on my mind, I said to her, "Let me be clear, you will not be working three jobs." If you are a woman, you may be a little incensed, as you read this. That would be because I broke a cardinal biblical rule. Proverbs 15:1

says, "Harsh words stir up anger..." Well, that is what I did, and our pleasant night took a turn for the worse.

So, we had our little spat, left at disagreeing, and she went on with what she was doing. In my mind, we were going to move past it. Yet, for some strange reason, I just could not let the argument go. During our disagreement she made some valid points, to which I conceded. She also clarified her intentions while sharing her perspective of the situation. Doing so left me with a peaceful understanding that things were not as bad as I initially believed. It was over, or at least it was supposed to be. However, I could not let it go. On the inside of me something terrible was going on: It was brewing and brewing and brewing. As it did, I became angrier and angrier and angrier. It was not violent anger, but the kind of anger that would not allow me to sleep. Now, I know the Bible says don't let the sun go down on your wrath (See Eph. 4:26), but I thought I was being silly and would be able to let it go. Why revisit the argument? We resolved the problem, right? That was my understanding at the time. Besides, I couldn't even figure out why I was angry anyway! So, I went to bed.

I awoke early the next day, and there it was, that feeling of anger. To make matters worse, as time went on, I started feeling insecure about our relationship. Now I was really beginning to wonder what was happening. I had been married for 14 years, and until that point in our marriage, I never struggled with insecurity. With all of this inner chaos breaking forth in my life I turned to God for answers. I needed to know why the anger and insecurity were there. So, I asked God to show me.

After asking Him what was going on, I had a few dreams. Those dreams unveiled my apathy in my marriage, my selfish sexual habits, and hurts that I received during the dating stages of our relationship. All of these contributed to my struggle with insecurity.

I will never forget one particular dream. In the dream, my fraternal twin brother and I were in bed with a woman between us. In the dream, I wanted to make love to her, and my brother just wanted to have sex with her. However, she chose me. It was an expression of her desire to simply be loved.

When my twin appears in my dreams, I have learned that he represents the other side of me. God was saying, "Kevin you are insecure because you treat your wife like a sex toy rather than a woman to be loved." He was showing me that meeting the needs of her heart would alleviate my worries of somebody else meeting them for me. He was unveiling the selfishness that was behind my tear.

In other dreams, he showed me that the insecurity was rooted in things that happened in my childhood. Who would have known that these things were hiding in my heart? Who would have known that something was in my heart that threatened the greatness of my marriage?

My dilemma may seem strange to some of you reading, while it may be familiar to others. Either way, it is an experience that most of us understand and Naaman is no different. Naaman, like myself, came to discover that something was very wrong in his heart. At first, we don't see the problem. Then God orchestrated an event that took the story in a new direction. In doing so, He taught us a great truth.

In the last chapter, I spoke of a prophetic act by the king of Israel. In the passage, Israel's king tore his robe after Naaman's personal issue became an international issue. He did so because Naaman's issue became the source of the tension in his life. His act was to be a revelation to onlookers regarding what was happening in his heart. His act was prophetic because it was forecasting what was about to happen in the life of Naaman. The revelation of this truth is what has allowed me to understand what God was doing in my situation with my wife, and how to best respond to it.

Tension Leads to Tearing

There is nothing in life as provocative as tension. It was the tension in my marriage that began my cycle of stress. But really, what is tension? How can we define it? In the last chapter, we introduced the idea that tension leads to tearing. I also made mention of the principle of the "commonplace." Now I want to define tension since it is at the heart of the "commonplace" idea. Tension results when two or more things add stress to a common point. As we briefly discussed in the last chapter, for tension to exist there must be a commonplace from which the two opposing forces originate. In my marriage, it was the common goal of integrating my wife back into the workforce. In the king's life, it was the button or thread of fabric that held his robe together. In America, it is the thought of making our country safe, providing affordable health care, and fair and equal treatment for all. And in Naaman's life, it was the shared desire of all parties to see him healed. He wanted to be healed. His wife and her servant's discussion centered around his healing. The king of Syria's goal in sending him to Israel was to get him healed. What is it in your life that you are trying to hold together? Whatever it is, just know that the presence of a shared goal causes tension in your life. That is important to remember. It is important because while it is a point of stress, it is also what keeps you connected. So, the problem is not the button or goal that holds you together. Likewise, people who do not recognize this reality disengage from the goal altogether, thus resulting in permanent separation. Though tension leads to tearing, it does not have to drive us to destruction.

Tearing Leads to Revelation

Now that conflict has torn you, how should you respond? As you ponder that for a second, I want you to really consider that this, in my opinion, is the most important question to answer. Why? It's the most important question to answer because it will govern your response. One thing about being torn is the reality that often we use the initial conflict to further the divide in our friendships, marriages, immediate and extended family relationships. Some people allow the conflict on their job to cause them to separate from their career. One thing about conflict that we must be wary of is the temptation to use tearing as an excuse for separation.

Now, I know, most people feel as though they have the right to throw away their relationships based on various degrees of conflict. To some extent that is true. There are definitely times when separation is inevitable. That being said, Jesus presents us with a challenge regarding conflict. His disciples also follow suit in their teachings about conflict.

Peter once asked Jesus regarding forgiveness, how many times he should forgive someone who offended him. Jesus then gave His classic answer, 70 times 7 (Matt. 18:22). He clearly tells us how to handle conflict in that passage. In another passage He said, "If you come to the altar and find there that your brother/sister has a problem with you, leave your gift at the altar and first be reconciled to your brother (Matt. 5:24). To further promote the idea of conflict resolution, He even challenged one of the most controversial subjects in the scriptures—marriage and divorce. Yet, He was not alone in His challenge to us regarding how to handle conflict. Those who walked alongside of Him have their own advice regarding how to handle conflict. The

Apostle Paul said over and over again in many places in his writings, "Be of one mind" or "Be of one spirit" (See Eph. 4:4, Phil. 4:4, I Cor. 12:13). James says in his book, "Do not speak evil of one another..." (See James 4:11-12) The beloved John also challenges our perspective on conflict. He said in 1 John 4:20, "How can you say that you love God whom you have not seen, but hate your brother whom you have seen." As you can see, there is a prevailing idea of resolving conflict woven throughout the scriptures.

Take it Personally

Let me ask the question again, how should "you" respond to conflict? I put "you" in quotes for a reason. That reason is that you would learn how to take it personally. What I mean by the phrase *take it personally* is this: If you went back to read the passages of scripture that deal with conflict you would see a prevailing idea. That idea is that conflict resolution is dependent on the person or persons involved in the conflict taking a personal stake in resolving the conflict. There is a scripture in Romans 12:18 which says, "As much as depends on (you) live peaceably with all men." I don't think I can make it any plainer than that.

The resolution of a conflict is dependent upon you taking a realistic look at what you contribute to the conflict. The truth is, conflict helps us to see who we are. It causes a revelation to unfold in our life.

In fact, Naaman had a revelation. It was about what was

going on in his heart. Something came up in him, and all hell broke loose. Were there other factors that contributed to his attitude and negative response to the man of God's instructions? Sure there were, and we will deal with that later. But as of now, I want you to consider that Naaman's response to the conflict was a personal decision—one that almost cost him his miracle. Now I want you to consider what conflict has revealed in you that may be keeping you from experiencing God's best for your life. Is it fear and insecurity, such as what was threatening my wife and I getting the most fulfillment out of our marriage? Maybe for you, there is conflict on your job. Maybe refusing to see your part in the conflict is hindering the promotion you so desire. Perhaps it is more profound than that for you or your country. Might the lack of a nation's economic greatness have something to do with its unwillingness to acknowledge how it contributes to the problem?

I know that looking at your self and being introspective is hard. Sometimes it is tough, and for me, it was sobering to think that there was some faulty idea hiding in my heart and threatening my marriage. So, I ask you the question that Jesus asked the man at the pool of Bethesda in John 5:6, "Do you want to be made well?" In previous chapters, I spoke of Naaman's admirable passion for pursuing his healing. Now he is at the door of opportunity. Everything he has been through has all led to this moment: the embarrassing blemish on his great reputation, the discussion between his wife and her servant, the financial strain on his nation's economy, the tension of war created by his nation's outlandish request. Was he really going to allow one conflict of opinion to cost him everything! Remember, he is a man of war, and it begs us to ask the question that he should have asked himself. 'Naaman, "Are you going to lose the war because of a miscalculation on the battlefield?"' What are you going to lose trying to be right! Do your self a favor and use conflict as an opportunity to take it personally and do a self-assessment of your heart. There is something behind that tear that God is revealing to you—about you!

Reflection Activity

- Take a moment to think about some of the conflicts in your life.

- Write down what you feel God is revealing to "you" about yourself? Remember, the thing revealed may be an improvement to your character, or it may be a flaw in it.

Chapter 6

It's All in How You See It

In the last chapter, I asked the question, "What are you going to lose trying to be right?" This question is important to consider. It should have caused you to look at your situation differently. It is a question that begs me to address the problem of vision and perspective. You see, Naaman's problem was not just leprosy. The real problem was his vision. I am a man of vision. I like to see visions. I like to talk about vision. I like to teach about vision. I even like to listen to the visions of others. But I have also come to know that often we confuse visions with dreams. If I asked you to define the difference would you be able to do so? Sometimes, the reason we confuse the two is because both are manifested visually. Though they may appear to us in similar ways, they are not the same.

Dreams

A dream is something that we see as a result of our desires. Ecclesiastic 5:3 says, that a dream may come from the busyness of the day. Isaiah 29:8 says of dreams (paraphrased), "As when a hungry man dreams and awakes still hungry." What I want you to see is desire manifested visually. For instance, Naaman had a dream, a desire to be healed. We know this to be true even though there was no mention of a dream in the passage. While there is no mention of a dream, we see evidence of it when he finds out from the Israeli slave girl that he can be whole. It was the idea of being whole that ignited his passion. Many of you reading this have had or will have an encounter with the right person that has the ability to inspire possibility in you. Dreams show us what is possible for our lives and future.

Visions

Visions, however, are different than dreams. Dreams show us the possibility of more. Visions show us the way forward. More importantly, it gives us the ability to see the finished product. I like to describe vision this way. Imagine that you are a passenger on a ship headed somewhere. The desire that helped to launch you into the deep was the dream; it is the idea of going somewhere. Yet, when the captain looks through his binoculars and sees his landing spot afar off, and determines that he wants to go in the direction of his prize, that, my friends, is vision. Dreams often lack direction. They are generally hopeful or wishful thinking, but vision is resolute. It has seen the end and has chartered a course to head in a specific direction. The ability to see the finished product is what Naaman lacked. He could not see his healing in the water.

It was his lack of vision that led him to a faulty conclusion regarding the situation. There he was standing at the door of opportunity, ready to see the fulfillment of his dream, when all of a sudden, he let the instructions regarding his healing offend him. You see, the problem was not with his ability to dream. I dare say that the same is true for many of you reading this book. The problem is your vision. Naaman could not see the healing in the dirty waters of the Jordan. Likewise, you may not see the healing for your marriage in doing date nights; you may not see the healing of your body in giving up your favorite foods: you may not see your promotion in praying, submitting, and serving that mean boss. Pastors, you may not see the healing of your church in allowing people to grow in their spiritual gifts. You only see what Naaman saw—the mess. Howbeit, the miracle was in that mess!

That is why I titled this chapter, "It's All In How You See It!" I did so to drive home the point that you, the Church, America, and other countries as well, are missing out on God's miracle all because you don't like the mess you have to go through to get it. My wife and I had some intense and awkward moments as God tore me open to show me who I was. At which point, I had to make a decision. Did I want to deal with past hurts and issues in my life that were threatening my future? Or, did I want to have the best marriage known to man? Did I want to deal with my mess to experience the miracle? How do you see it?

I want you to come away from this chapter knowing that dreaming of your miracle is not enough. It is not enough to wishfully imagine being more. It is not enough to merely want to be better. Dreams must ultimately lead to vision. A hope of a better marriage must lead to your ability to visualize that better marriage. A promise of a new career must go beyond fantasy. It must become a reality in your mind. I cannot stress this enough. Fantasizing about more will not sustain you when you have to get dirty to get it.

There was a miracle waiting for Naaman. There was a fulfillment of his desire waiting in the dirty Jordan waters. Your miracle just may be in a place that makes you uncomfortable. If you are merely living on wishful thinking, you will not be able to see your dream fulfilled. On the other hand, if you can see the end goal, the dirtiest and most uncomfortable places will not deter you from getting what God has for you.

I want you to think about dreams and visions this way: Dreams inspire us to run, but visions inspire us to stay the course. In other words, vision sustains us. Proverbs 29:18 says it this way, "Where there is no vision, the people perish." According to this verse, the only people dying short of the goal line are those who can't see insightfully.

Therefore, I encourage you to open your eyes and see what is before you. When walking with God you must learn that He often puts big blessings in a small places. So as you chase your dream remember that obtaining it has everything to do with the fact that it is all in how you see it.

Reflection Activity

- Take a moment and consider what you have to gain from being obedient and doing something different.

- Now consider what you have to lose. Remember, Naaman was a great and honorable man. What great man wants to wallow in the mud? None! He had something to lose, but his miracle was in those muddy waters. So, while he had something to lose he also had more to gain. Take this time to meditate on what you have to gain from doing something unconventional.

- Make a list based on the last activity. Identify the problem, then list the pros and cons.

For example:

Problem: Naaman had to wash in dirty water to be healed of his condition.

Pros: healing, full night of sleep, respect of his troops, improved self-image

Con: sickness, pain, family disunity, possible forced early retirement, vulnerable to attack

Chapter 7

The More Eyes the Better

The Bible says in Proverbs 11:14, "In the multitude of counselors there is safety." Proverbs 15:22 also says, "Plans fail for lack of counsel, but with many advisors they succeed." In other words, it is suggested to us that there are times in our life when we cannot see things clearly by ourself. I am hardly one to dispense advice on this subject, but it is true. At some point, all of us need help seeing life correctly. Sometimes God has to remind me of the importance of having people in my life. Having the ability to hear Him so clearly means that He is generally my Counselor. Sometimes this results in me flying solo. I know that this is not a good thing, but it has been that way for years. What I have discovered the hard way, however, is that God also uses people to help move you into His promises. He used Moses to establish Joshua. He used Elijah to establish Elisha. He used Eli to establish Samuel. Finally, He used David to establish Solomon. It is true that God uses people!

The question is why? God uses people to help us see what we cannot see by ourselves. This is what happened to Naaman. God placed unlikely counselors in Naaman's life. There he was angrily going in the opposite direction of his miracle when unsuspecting voices challenged his thinking. They said, "Master, if the man had asked you to do something great, would you not have done it?" How much more then when he says wash and be clean?" In other words, they were saying to him, "Are you going to go home angry and still have leprosy? Are you going to miss this opportunity for a miracle all because of the condition of the water?" They challenged his rationale. That is what we all need from time to time—someone who sees things differently. Someone who can help us get to the right conclusion.

Naaman was willing to go home angry. The reality, however, is that no degree of emotion was going to change his situation. You should also know that no matter how angry you are at the conflict in your life, no matter how sad, or depressed, or overwhelmed you are, not one of those emotions is going to improve your situation. I know this is not what some people want to hear. We have become a people of empathy. We carefully watch every word from our mouth so that we do not offend anyone. Still, the reality is that sometimes we need people in our life that will not be intimidated by our status or our raging emotions. Sometimes we need these kinds of people to get in our face and challenge us to live; to try to save our marriages and our careers; to try to make a country great. Sometimes, it is hard to see that those who challenge us to experience God's best are not trying to hurt us but help us. Naaman's servants were trying to help their master see the situation clearly. They caught the vision and were trying to open his eyes to the opportunity to see his dream fulfilled. Who in your life has permission to challenge the way you think about your situation? Are they right? Have you even considered the possibility that they are right? Maybe you and your spouse can reconcile. Perhaps you and your wayward child can come together again. Maybe there is a better job than the one you have. Can you see the possibility of change, and if not, are there trustworthy people in your life that can help you do so?

The Right Kind of Counselors

There is another interesting thing about the relationship between Naaman and the servants. It was the status differences that caught my attention. This particular aspect of the story is critical to understand. Notice that God did not put kings and other commanders in Naaman's journey to wholeness. He placed servants—people in humble life circumstances. Just think about it, Naaman took advice from these people. Can you imagine? The equivalent would be a government employee sticking his nose into the President's staff meeting and offering his opinion. If you think it is an outlandish idea to consider today, then just think about the risk these servants took by speaking out of turn in this period in history. They took a serious risk, but it was necessary.

Here is something intriguing to note, God placed the humility Naaman needed to achieve his dream in his servants. They could give him good advice because they understood humility. As servants they also understood being humiliated. Naaman, however, did not. This teaches us something noteworthy. It teaches us to be open to the advice of people we might lightly regard. They just might hold the keys to your miracle. You see, if Naaman had taken his concerns to his king or another commander, it is highly likely that they would have agreed with his point of view. It is entirely possible that they would have advised him according to his pride and appealed to his sense of dignity and reputation. That, however, has its roots in the truth that they do not understand humility either. It was a matter of perspective. Bishop Jakes pointed out in one of his teachings that the turtle does not have the same point of view as the giraffe. Naaman was a giraffe who needed to be able to see what the turtles saw. Therefore, God intentionally placed in his midst those who knew what it took to get what he was after. To them, as servants, there was nothing outrageous about bathing in dirty water. They know what it is to keep things in perspective.

Keeping things in perspective means that we must pay attention and trust that God has put the right counselors in our life. It also means that we must be able to recognize good counsel. It was the counsel of those who related to where he was trying to go that had the most significant impact on him achieving his dream. Likewise, you do not need to take up things such as your marital concerns with your friends who have either never been married or despise marriage. The last thing a marriage in conflict needs is someone to encourage the tension. As I stated earlier, tension can lead to tearing.

Be Teachable

There is an interesting dichotomy in this text as it relates to counseling. We all know that Naaman eventually achieved his dream of being healed. We also know that his healing is in part the result of the excellent counsel given by his servants. What I find interesting, though, is the fact that he was willing to take advice from his servants, but not from Elisha's servant. Both provided him with excellent counsel that would have helped him realize his dream. However, he was angry about Elisha's servant giving him advice. What this teaches us is the power of humility and the importance of being teachable.

If you have followed my ministry any length of time, you know that I specialize in teaching about the voice of God. I can teach this subject from just about any angle at this point in my life. This is yet another time when I think it is important to bring up this subject. Naaman had a word from God Almighty. However, he was resistant to what he heard all because of the vessel God chose to use. What I find more interesting is the fact that God did accommodate Naaman's ignorance by speaking to more reputable persons. When all was said and done, he still had to take instruction from a servant.

This reminds me of Balaam in Numbers 22-23. He took the wrong approach to earning money. By doing so, he angered God, and an angel was sent to take his life. When the angel appeared to do his job, the donkey Balaam was riding turned aside to protect its master. In doing so, the donkey hindered the angel from fulfilling his assignment. In response to the donkey's disobedience, Balaam struck the donkey. Howbeit, the donkey did it again. And again Balaam hit the donkey. Finally, God opened the spiritual eyes of Balaam. Then Balaam finally saw what the donkey saw. Then God opened the mouth of the donkey, and it said to Balaam, "Have I ever... before." The donkey challenged Balaam to consider the faithfulness of its service to him. He was also questioning why Balaam challenged his direction. Ultimately, the donkey was trying to give guidance to the prophet. But like Naaman, it is hard to take advice from someone perceived as beneath you.

Is it possible that the only thing keeping you from your miracle is the packaging of God's gift? Is it possible that His voice came to you in a way that you lightly regarded? This has two applications for the church today. One, it applies to those who think themselves too high to receive from those beneath them. It speaks of those we deem uneducated; or not as talented; not as reputable; not as civilized; and or not as intelligent as us. Two, this applies to a lot of those in the modern church who refuse to acknowledge that God still speaks to us directly—more specifically, in dreams and visions. Is it possible that your pizza dream contained the instructions that would have led you to the water where your dream was to be realized? Naaman despised the method whereby God provided the miracle. Likewise, his pride and unteachable spirit almost cost him his dream.

There is so much to say about this subject. When I think of Jesus and the Jews, I am reminded of this principle again. We often have a hard time receiving from God when He does not come in the package that we deem acceptable. Isaiah said something interesting about the coming of Jesus. He said that when we see Him, we would not see anything beautiful about Him (Isa. 53:2). I know that thoughts of Jesus spur images of a good-looking Greek man with a perfectly sculpted body hanging on a cross. However, Isaiah said that beauty would not be a principle characteristic of His person.

Some of you may not even realize the significance of Isaiah's description of the coming King. All throughout the book of 1st and 2nd Kings and 1st and 2nd Chronicles, you will see what seems to be a prerequisite for being king in Israel; that prerequisite was beauty. King Saul was more handsome and taller than any man in Israel, according to the scriptures (See I Sam. 9:2). King David was also described as "good-looking" (See 1 Sam. 16:12). His traitorous son, Absalom, was likewise described as "good-looking" and there was an emphasis on the beauty of his hair (2 Sam. 14:25). Just looking at this you might think to yourself, "How vain was Israel to put such a high value on the outer appearance of the king." I thought the same thing until I realized that God was the one choosing them. (See Daniel 2:21, 4:17) So it seemed quite customary to have a good-looking king. Then there was Jesus, the not so attractive King. Furthermore, please note that neither the scriptures nor any biblical writer describe Jesus as gorgeous. God did not package this King the same way He packaged previous kings. Likewise, Israel did not receive Him.

Not only did He not fit the norm of the "good-looking king," but He also did not meet the standards of other well-regarded prerequisites. He was not a Scribe or a Pharisee, the regarded religious scholars of that time. He was born in what was considered the ghetto of Israel. His stepfather married a woman who was with child before marriage. He hung out with prostitutes, tax collectors, and other sinners. He did not fit the mold, and they rejected Him for it. Rejecting Him meant rejecting the voice of God in their lives. These are in fact, all of the things about which they questioned Him. They asked Him where He got His authority since He was not of the Levitical priesthood (See Mark 11:28). They questioned the source of His wisdom and knowledge

(See Matt 13:54). They called into question His authenticity because He allowed sinners to touch Him (See Luke 5:27-32, 7:39). And guess what? We are still doing the same thing today. We reject preachers who are not from our part of town. We reject things not produced to our standards such as books, movies, and music. We reject good men and women of God because they did not go to a Bible college. We reject good people God gives as potential spouses because they do not look a certain way. We reject God's blessings to us through people who are of a different race. We do a good job of derailing our own blessings because God did not package it the way we deem acceptable. Are you missing Jesus because He is not coming to you well packaged? Naaman almost missed the miracle because he did not like how God delivered the message. Be teachable!

The idea of Naaman being unteachable further leads us to the conclusion that Naaman was selfish and uncompromising. It is hard to learn from others when everything in your world revolves around you!

Just think about it for a second, the slave girl put her life at risk making a statement that she could not support. The reality is that God and Elisha owed Naaman nothing. What would have happened to her if Elisha had refused to heal Naaman? Not only that, but also the servants put their lives in their own hands speaking out of turn. Also, we can consider the king of Syria who provided resources for Naaman to pay for his healing. Then there was the obvious possibility of war if the king of Israel refused Naaman's request. Lastly, there was also Elisha, who was at home when this request came to his doorstep. Look at all of these people who were inconvenienced by Naaman. And to think, he dared to walk away from his dream because he did not like the instructions. How selfish!

Who have you inconvenienced? How is your uncompromising attitude offending those who sacrificed for you to have the opportunity to achieve your dream? Naaman was not teachable because he could not consider another person's point of view. That being said, he could not consider another point of view because he was selfish. Again, be teachable!

Managing Expectations

One good thing about healthy counseling relationships is the prospect of helping you to manage your expectations. One thing the servants did was ask a provocative question. They said, "Master, if the man of God had asked you to do some great thing, would you not have done it? Then how much more when he says wash and be clean." By asking this question, they made Naaman think about the same water differently. That, my friends, is good counseling. Good counseling helps you to see the same thing differently. They essentially said, "Dude, let's think about this again. Are you really going to walk away from this life-changing opportunity!"

Don't Ask Me to Fix the Problem

Managing expectations is a critical idea to tackle. What we see as we look at this story is that Naaman's biggest problem was his inability to manage his expectations. There are more than a few places where the heart of the conflict centers around what Naaman thought would happen. We see it first when Naaman's issue hits the international stage. The king of Israel, upon receiving the king of Syria's letter, immediately expresses his discontentment with the situation. At the heart of his issue was Naaman's expectation of the king to bring healing to his situation. The obvious problem with this scenario is rooted in the idea that Naaman came to see a man about fixing an issue no man could fix.

Does that sound familiar? Have you placed the power to see your dream fulfilled; your marriage healed; your children return home; the sustainability of your job, etc. on the shoulders of another human being? That is called a misplaced expectation. It is common for us to think more highly of the visible people in our life than we do about the divine invisible person in our life. Likewise, as you can see, Naaman's expectation was the catalyst to the conflict in the life of the king. Can I tell you that you do your family, friends, and even sometimes your boss, a disservice when you ask them to shoulder your need for a miracle? Sure, they can pray for you. They can give you a couple of dollars here and there. They can take you back and forth to your appointments with your oncologist. But they cannot fix what is wrong in your life. That responsibility belongs solely to God. Now, it is true that God works through people. God eventually worked through Elisha to resolve the issue, but it must remain ever so clear to us that God alone can rectify the problem.

Why is this idea so important to embrace? Well for starters, it takes a lot of stress out of the relationship when the other person is allowed to be human too. Naaman's expectation of the king of Israel was almost enough to take the two countries to war. Is there a war in your relationship because you have expectations of the other person—expectations that you should place on God?

Treat Me Right

Not only did Naaman have a misplaced expectation in his relationship to others, but he also had a misplaced expectation of how he should be treated. The lofty idea of special treatment in relationships is an issue that has caused more than a few problems. There Naaman was standing at the door of opportunity. He had traveled from his own country to see a change in his life. When he finally arrived at that place in his life, he realized that God put his miracle in the hands of a man. This is where we need balance. God did not limit Himself to the hands of the prophet. The miracle, in fact, was not in the hand of the man of God, but in the water God empowered. As I said previously, we cannot look to man for our answer. We must look to God because man is often only a conduit or even a sign to direct you to the place of the miracle.

With that said, the man of God's response triggered something in Naaman. Instead of coming to the door and greeting the great commander, Elisha chose to send his servant to deliver the message. In the federal government, it is uncommon for a non-supervisory employee to give direction to a senior level manager. Generally, these managers speak among themselves to provide guidance. Well, that is what we have taking place here. We have a very respected military man and a highly regarded prophetic voice meeting on different levels. In Naaman's mind, the proper protocol would have been for Elisha to greet him and instruct him. When this did not happen, the text says that Naaman said, "I thought to myself that he would greet me and wave his hand over me and I would be healed."

What Naaman's thoughts reveal to us is his expectation of special treatment. He thought highly of himself. He also had an idea of how others should see him as well. After all, even the text opens by describing his exceptional status. I am confident that his fame and reputation as a conqueror had spread to other countries; that would also include Israel. Maybe it didn't. Either way, in Naaman's mind it did.

The real truth of this particular idea is that conflict is often rooted in the notion of ego—who we are, how we think we should be treated, and how others should see us is often the enemy of successful relationships.

Care-filled Counsel

Here is a word for all those who endeavor to be channels of God's counsel; how you minister God's goodness is just as important as getting the job done. Sometimes we are so goal oriented that we inadvertently forget that we are dealing with people. I am most certainly guilty of this. Sometimes I view people as projects that need fixing; thereby ignoring that they are people with feelings. In doing so, I often complete my God-given assignments and walk away with a sense of fulfillment. On the other hand, usually, the person I treated like a project is hurt by my abrupt departure from their life.

I was not aware of how severe this issue was in my life until I lost of my best friends. I learned through the experience that while love will make people put up with your foolishness, it will also make them protect themselves from it as well.

Naaman was upset with Elisha in our passage, and it was wholly justified. I know that most people preach this passage with the intent of making Naaman the sole cause of the unpleasantness in the text. However, in doing so, they neglect the reality that Elisha is the catalyst for everything that follows after their initial meeting. It was how the man of God handled the ministry opportunity that ignited and fueled the conflict. Having taken notice of this in the text, God spoke to me clearly and said, "Kevin, how you do what you do is just as important as getting it done!"

Providing care-filled counsel means that we must remember that we are dealing with people. I once prepared a sermon for my preaching class based on the seven last words of Christ. My assigned topic was anguish. It came from Matthew 27:46 when Jesus said, "My God, My God, why have You forsaken Me." It was my goal to communicate how to survive seasons of anguish in life. As I sought God about the insights He wanted me to preach from the passage, He said, "Tell them to be human." I thought it was an interesting statement. He wanted me to relay to the audience that it is okay to be human.

Naaman, as impressive as he was; as powerful as he was; was still a human. Likewise, no matter how great the people we minister to may be, they are still human. Some of you will minister to presidents and stand before kings. In such instances, it is easy to assume that the greatness of the position means that those who occupy them have strong character. We falsely believe that they are superhuman. But at the end of the day, they are just like you and me, human. President Trump is a human. Former presidents, to include Barak Obama, are humans. The generals of great armies, great dads, and husbands, great mothers, and wives, great leaders, pastors, and CEOs, are all human. That being the case, ministering effectively to people requires that we remember their humanity.

Choosing to acknowledge the humanity of others is important to remember so that we do not further the pain in someone's life through our casual ministry. At a minimum,

Elisha could have come to the door and greeted the man. I have heard people make a lot of judgmental statements about Naaman's response without considering whether or not his response was warranted. Let me say that his response, though founded on an improper expectation, was justified. Later I will show you why. I will show you that God was not only exposing the pride in Naaman, but also in His servant Elisha.

Let me say to those who desire counsel; while it is not okay to place the expectation of fixing your problems at the feet of humans, it is okay to expect humane treatment. I have seen people counsel with such harsh and judgmental attitudes that they were more damaging than helpful. On one occasion, I rescued a woman from a toxic counseling encounter. The woman who caused the damage called herself a prophet. Her words broke down a fragile woman. So, I rebuked the prophet for her inhumane treatment. Good counsel resolves problems, not adds to them.

Just consider that both Naaman and Elisha's servants gave the commander the same advice. The servant of the man of God said, "Wash and be clean." Naaman's servants, likewise, encouraged him to wash and be clean. What was the difference? Why did he respond to one and not the other? I believe it was because of the way the word was delivered. Elisha sent his sympathy to the door via his servant. But Naaman's servants took the time required to reason with him until he was comfortable.

That leads to another idea that I would like to highlight. One reason Naaman's servants were so encouraging and effective in getting him to his dream had to do with the fact that they knew him. Elisha, on the other hand, had only heard of him. The difference was relationship! Naaman's servants had been on the journey with him. They were there when he returned home in pain. They were there when his family was discussing his issue. They were there when he got the word that healing was possible. They were there when the king of Syria signed the documents that created a path to see his dream fulfilled. They were there when the man of God treated him poorly. The point is, they were with him the whole time. They stood by him in his ups and downs. It is also clear that they cared about Naaman because they invested time developing a relationship with him.

How do I know they cared? Well, for starters they had nothing to lose by keeping their mouths shut. Their advice did not change their status as servants. That means that something compelled them to care about a man they referred to as master—not father, not brother, but master! Think about that for a second.

An excellent counselor cares about seeing you achieve your dream. That being said, one thing that makes a counselor a better counselor is caring enough about people to not only do the job, but to do it with care.

Reflection Activity:

- Identify and make a list of people in your life that meet the criteria of good counselors.

- Take the time to consider counseling if you have severe issues that are holding you back from being successful in specific areas of your life.

- Take a moment and consider whether or not your expectations are properly grounded in God, not in people.

For Counselors

- If you are a counselor, think about whether or not you are doing your job with care, or just doing the job.

- Consider what you can do to ensure that you counsel with care? For example, you might consider praying before each session. Or choosing a less stressful environment to hold meetings. Maybe you can consider giving yourself a "cool down" period before starting. Whatever method you choose, just think about how to improve your ability to empathize with the counselee.

Chapter 8

Four Types of Conflict

As stated in the introduction, conflict is a reality that we must embrace. Again, Jesus said conflict is a natural part of life's narrative. Therefore, we should consider the weight of His words. If He says that conflict is a part of life, then it is a part of the experience we call life. For that reason, God directed me to write this book. He wants me to teach you how to live and thrive from conflict, instead of allowing it to destroy your life and the lives of those around you.

I have said a lot about conflict, but what is it? If we are going to learn to thrive in the midst of it, then we should start by defining it. Conflict is defined as disagreement; an argument; a clashing together. Conflict occurs when two things moving in the opposite direction make contact with each other. For instance, science tells us that the collision of cold air and warm air masses result in a storm. It is possible for storms to form in your life when things come together that don't mix well. Our main passage, for example, is filled with conflicting ideas.

First, it starts by presenting us with a sick soldier. Then the slave girl advises her sick master. Next, we realize that the people with the power to fulfill his dream are from the very place he raided to get the slave girl. There was a conflict between the kings, a conflict between the king of Israel and the prophet, a conflict between the prophet and Naaman, a conflict in the instructions, a conflict in theological ideas; there was conflict. Things came together in a way that resulted in a storm.

Likewise, a faithful spouse can be met with a cheating spouse. A first-time mother can be met with a stillborn baby. A life-long friendship can be met with betrayal. A life of healthy eating and exercise can be met with cancer. That is what happened to my mother. After years of eating correctly and taking care of herself, she received a cancer diagnosis. I once had a friend who died right after his new bride got pregnant. I, myself, was furloughed twice one month after buying a new car. Life happens, and when contrary things come together in our life, the result is conflict. Any number of things can collide in your life and turn it upside down in an instant.

When we ponder Naaman's story we learn a few things about conflict. One being that conflict falls into four main categories. They are:

- Circumstantial Conflict
- Relational Conflict
- Internal Conflict
- Ideological Conflict

Circumstantial Conflict

Circumstantial conflict occurs when the circumstances in our life clash with each other. Naaman had a clash in his circumstances. There he was ready to obtain the dream he traveled so far to apprehend when the man of God told him that his dream of being healed would manifest in a dirty river. Can you imagine looking at the water and it is so dirty that you would rather go home without the fulfillment of your dream? Is there a dirty river standing in the way of the dream God has for your life?

Maybe you are like Naaman as well. Just think about it. Not only were there conflicting differences in the water, there were also personal conflicts; Folks, Naaman was a sick soldier! Are there circumstances in your life that are coming together in a way that makes you want to detract from pursuing greatness? Maybe the better question for all of us is, how thirsty are you? How bad do you want to see your dream fulfilled?

I Prefer that Water over There

"Why that water?" Naaman asked. This statement takes us back to the issue of perspective. Naaman did not have a problem with the method. He had a problem with the solution. I think most of us can agree that water, whether dirty or clean, is still water. Notice that he did not fight for some other method, though he had one in mind. His argument was about the water. His question was, "Why this water and not that water over there." Doesn't it sound ridiculous when stated that way?

There are a lot of things I have the pleasure of doing for God. One is convincing people to be open to His mysterious way of doing things. Please know that He is not committed to fulfilling His promises in ways that we expect. My warning to those of you with hidden prejudices is that you abandon such ideas. You never know when your life will hang in the balances of a skin complexion, weight difference, or gender difference that you do not consider favorable. That is called a conflict of circumstances.

Imagine needing a kidney from a donor whose blood you despise. What do you do when your life is hinged to this person? How thirsty can you be if you allow the silly idea of "I prefer this water over that water" to permeate your thinking?

I watched a video on social media one day of a lady who denied her son access to medical attention. She did so because she did not agree with the ethnicity of the attending doctor. It was a "Naaman" water situation. She wanted to be satisfied by her choice of water. The water (doctor) the hospital provided was not good enough. I thought to myself, "How silly and unfortunate. This woman is willing to allow her child to suffer because she does not agree with the skin tone of the doctor."

There are other applications of this truth regarding "choice of water." For instance, I shall forever be in awe of the number of people who are single because they have not met "their type." Let me give some much-needed advice to my single readers. God does not care about your type. I was not my wife's type. She was not my type. Nonetheless, we have been married 15 years as of August 2, 2018. Likewise, we can both report that we are experiencing the best relationship of our lives. Why am I bringing this up? Well for starters, it is an excellent example of how we miss our miracle because we don't like God's choice of water for our lives. Furthermore, it is an excellent example of clashing circumstances: it is the moment that God introduces a single person to someone who is not their type.

There are other examples I could use as well that illustrate conflict in the circumstances. One biblical illustration that comes to mind is the time Jesus sent His disciples in a boat to the other side of the sea (Matt. 14:22-23, Mark 6:45-52). The Bible records that when they were in the middle of the sea that the winds and waves were contrary. This means that the boat they were in and the winds and waves were going in opposite directions. In fact, there was so much conflict and opposition in their circumstances that it says that they were straining at rowing. But what I appreciate about them so much is the fact that they kept rowing in spite of the opposition to their direction. They too had a choice before them. They could have gone back to the shore from which they left. Or, they could have gone forward to reach the shore ahead of them. What we see here is the same idea, "this water, or that water over there." It always boils down to how bad you want it?"

Naaman wanted to be clean, but he had to get clean in a dirty place. Isn't that an oxymoron? How does a person get clean in a dirty place? Again, a better question to ask is how bad do you want what God has for you?

Naaman even offered up a better solution; one that made sense in light of the circumstances. He said in verse 12, "Is not Abanah and the Pharpar, the rivers of Damascus, better than all the waters of Israel?" What he means is, "If I want to be clean shouldn't I wash in clean waters."

It is this same rationale that plagues some of us today. We say, "Lord, shouldn't we do this instead?" Most of the time, our dissatisfaction with God's solution has everything to do with the conflict in the circumstances.

Relational Conflict

The next type of conflict that we see in Naaman's story is "relational" conflict. This type of conflict is the result of dueling persons. When we consider the idea of conflicting circumstances, we realize what makes it preferable to relational conflict. Relational conflict is challenging because it puts the potential for blame on both parties. Not so with circumstantial conflict because it results from the collision of things outside of our control. Relational conflict, however, is entirely about our role in the conflict. For instance, if your car breaks down and you are late for work, it is normal to place the blame on the car. This is often the case, even though the breakdown may be due to your negligence in caring for the vehicle. In such a case, it is easy to avoid dealing with your part in causing the problem. However, if you are late for work because of a carpool member, then everything changes. All of a sudden, one of the two of you is to blame. The conflict is the result of someone's failure to take responsibility for the problem. For this reason, relational conflict often results in a need for reconciliation.

Today, there is more relational conflict than one can fathom. In August of 2017, a group of racists and anti-racist protestors feuded. Watching it play out on the television in the year 2017 was surreal. The result of that day proved tragic for a young woman. It proved to be more tragic as it became clear that America was deeply divided and hurting.

It became even more intense as President Trump made

remarks that people found offensive. There were some who thought he was wrong and others who thought he was right. The situation resulted in blogs and video rebuttals arguing the case for both sides. People took such a firm stance on their position that they even went as far as severing ties with those who held a different point of view.

Then there was the next major American crisis of 2017, Hurricane Harvey. Hurricane Harvey came through Texas and dropped in a span of a few days a record amount of rainfall. In fact, it dropped all of what the state typically received in a year in a short span of time. The flooding was record-setting for our country. In the midst of the chaos, people were devastated. The governor of Texas did not foresee that the situation would be so dire. Therefore, he chose not to evacuate the city. The result was unimaginable, and many people required rescuing.

While all of this was happening, a Pastor of a famous mega-church in the area responded slower than expected. Or, at least that is what the news reported. Consequently, the backlash of hate towards this man of God was horrendous. Likewise, people took sides, and relational conflicts sprung up everywhere.

I remember reading one particular social media post. A guy made known to one of the groups I am a part of, that he unfriended a friend. It was not an unfriending due to something crazy. It was an unfriending due to opposing opinions about the issue. Can you believe that? The guy did not sleep with his wife. He did not cause him bodily harm. He did not even rob him. He just took a different position on the matter.

In our text, we see several relational conflicts. First, we see this type of challenge between the two kings. When the king of Syria sent Naaman to the king of Israel, it was assumed by the king of Israel that the Syrian king was instigating a war. Then there was the relational conflict between the king of Israel and Elisha, the man of God. When Elisha got word of the distress the Israeli king was under, he took offense. He said, "Why have you torn your robe? Send him to me that he may know that there is a prophet in Israel."

The most regarded of the relational conflicts, however, was between Naaman and the man of God. There Naaman stood at the door waiting to see what God had in store for him. He had traveled far to see his dream fulfilled. Then when he arrived, the man of God sent his servant to the door with instructions that Naaman considered preposterous. At that moment the relationship between the two changed to one of hostility.

At the Heart of Conflict

One thing that looms large in the conflicts I mentioned is pride. Yes, I said pride! It was pride that made one king assume that he could impose his native's problems on another nation. It was pride that upset the man of God. For again, he said, "Send him to me that he may know that there is

a prophet in Israel." Notice the expectation of notoriety in the man of God's statement. Finally, it was the pride in Naaman's heart that led to him walking away in anger.

A lot of theologians look at this passage and focus on the apparent person, Naaman. They read where the scripture says that he, being angered by Elisha's response, turned away in anger. What they do not see is the subtle pride in the heart of the man of God.

To see what God showed me we have to look at Elisha's history. First, in 2 Kings 2:23-24, children teased him as he passed by them. Instead of walking away and ignoring their immaturity, he chose to curse them. The result was the death of 42 of them.

Then there was the incident in 2 Kings 4:8-37, in which he prayed for a barren woman to conceive a child. He did so in response to her kindness towards him. As a result, God honored his request, and she gave birth a year later. After some time, the child became sick and died. Therefore, she sought the counsel of the man of God. When she found him, he was sitting on a hill. Then he did something familiar to Naaman's story. He sent his servant to meet with her. His job was to assess the situation. So the servant did just that, but she wanted to speak to the man of God. Therefore, she lied to the servant and declared that everything in her life was fine. When she finally arrived at the feet of the man of God he said, "Leave her alone. She is in pain, and the Lord has hidden it from me." (2 Kings 5:27)

So, get the picture; Here is a ministry opportunity to which he sent his servant. Then he made the arrogant assumption that God hides nothing from him. He soon discovered that the child was dead.

In the next incident, we see further indications of his pride and arrogance. The woman, having unveiled her heart, is looking for a response from Elisha. He responded by sending his servant to minister to the dead child. He told him to lay his (Elisha's staff) on the head of the child. Hence the servant did so, but the child remained dead. Imagine that! It did not work as he thought it would. So here is an opportunity to minister, first, to meet with a woman in pain and second, to raise her child back to life, and in both situations, he relinquished his responsibility to someone else. Also, notice that he did so, not out of fear, but out of an over-inflated sense of self—in other words, pride!

Then we see his pride in the passage regarding Naaman. Again, I remind you that his only objective in seeing Naaman healed, as stated by the text, was to advance his reputation as Israel's prophet.

What I found interesting though, was how God humbled the man of God in every situation. He also humbled him in Naaman's story. Though Elisha intended for Naaman to realize that there was a prophet in Israel, 1 Kings 5:15 says that Naaman came to know that there was a God in Israel. Hallelujah!

This all brings us back to the relational conflict between

Naaman and Elisha. Having a complete profile of the man of God gives the text a completely different understanding. Now it does not seem that the source of the relational conflict is one-sided. Now we can see the pride in the man of God that became the source of the conflict. I know some preachers will not like this. Nonetheless, the truth is that many conflicts in the Church today stem from the pride in the heart of the servants of God.

Here the man of God was standing before a ministry opportunity, and he chose to abdicate it to his servant. Might the conflict in your marriage have to do with more than the person who seems to be the apparent problem? Maybe you have a tad bit of a part in the conflict.

Now, Elisha's weak reaction to the ministry moment does not excuse Naaman's behavior. I said it earlier, how bad do you want the dream God has for you if something as simple as the choice of waters deters you? Naaman's response was obviously due to his pride. He apparently thought that he should be treated like royalty. His reasoning takes us back to the section on managing expectations. One reason he was so offended was because pride made him entertain thoughts outside of reasonable expectations.

As you go forward with becoming whole and obtaining your greatness, I hope you are reasonable. If you haven't discovered the humanity of the servants of God, you will. And if you are prideful in your expectations, you can expect to be disappointed every single time.

One thing you should know about pride is that it blinds you to the truth. Just think about it. What made Elisha make the same mistake of missing the ministry moment twice? What made Naaman believe that the type of water was more important than the fulfillment of his dream? It was pride! The Bible says in Proverbs 14:12, "There is a way that seems right to a man whose end is destruction." See, sometimes it seems right to "us" and because "we" think it is right we are blinded to the destruction that awaits us.

How many great marriages and friendships have ended because of an argument about who was right? How many times did we seem right in our point of view? You see, pride makes us think we are so right that we cannot consider another person's point of view. That is why Naaman almost lost his dream.

Internal Conflict

The next to last type of conflict I see in Naaman's story is internal conflict. Internal conflict occurs when we have ideas that clash within us. This type of conflict usually manifests in the rambling of our inner voice. In my opinion, giving our attention to this type of conflict is critical. It is my persuasion that God allows the circumstantial conflicts and relational conflicts to show us our internal conflicts.

Earlier in this book, I told you that tension in our life leads to tearing and tearing leads to the exposure of hidden things. Remember, the king tore his robe in response to the king of Syria's imposing request to heal Naaman. The tearing of the robe revealed something more profound underneath. Also, the agony and stress of a possible war became visible in his reaction of tearing his robe. It was so evident, that Elisha said, "Why do you tear your robe..." Elisha knew that the conflict on the outside was a sign of a battle on the inside.

That is one of the primary purposes of this book, to get you to allow conflict to reveal what is hiding in you. Remember, you might find that conflict reveals a hero hiding in you as it did for David. Or, you might find hiding in your heart a coward like his brothers. Either way, the ultimate benefit of conflict is that it reveals what is hiding in our heart. Later, I will deal with why this is so important for us to take seriously.

As we look at Naaman's story, we can see that his circumstantial conflict led to the relational conflict, and ultimately created an internal conflict. I should also mention that it was the internal conflict that revealed the real source of his inability to obtain his dream. Look at what he said, "And I said to myself, surely he will come out and greet me and wave his hand over me, and I would be healed." Look at this grandiose expectation from someone he had never met. He even had a plan worked out for how God should fix the problem.

The Good Part of Him is Revealed Too

The good thing about his inner thoughts is that it revealed that he had faith. I tell people often that real faith sees. Though it does not see with the physical eyes, it most certainly sees something. Hebrews 11:27 says, Moses endured as **seeing** Him that is invisible. Verse 13 says, speaking of the early Israelite patriarchs, "And **seeing** afar off..."

How do we know that Naaman had faith? We know this because what he said to himself revealed that he had been imagining (seeing) how God was going to fix his problem. He came ready to get his miracle, but he thought it would manifest the way he saw it. Even though his expectations were flawed, I applaud the fact that he had enough faith to see it happening with the eyes of his heart.

I point this out to you to show you that even though conflict might reveal a problem in your heart. It can also highlight the good parts of it as well. I believe that every time God confronts evil in us, He also finds a redeeming quality too. I think having this balance of truth is essential. It is essential because it keeps us from falling prey to guilt and condemnation. This also means that we should seek to do the same in our conflicts with others. Though conflict may bring out the worst in a person, look for the good in them also. Doing so makes it easier for the person to take an honest look at himself or herself. There is nothing worse than feeling like everything you do is wrong; Hence the need for us to respond appropriately.

The Inner Conflict No One Likes to Discuss

There is a type of inner conflict that the church does not like to talk about today. It is a type of inner conflict that does not appear in the text, but it does appear in the lives of many people. There are inner conflicts where we have battles in our own heart. There are also inner spiritual conflicts where our spirit battles another spirit. That means that we need to deal with the topic of demons. Yes, I said demons!

Demons are spirits with ill intent. That is why they are called "evil" spirits. The word spirit in the Hebrew is *"ruach,"* and in Greek, it is *"pneuma."* They both mean wind or breath. They are the ideas behind our English words inspiration and motivation. That means that evil spirits are beings that inspire or motivate us to do evil things.

Today, the church has come to believe that Christians are exempt from the indwelling presence of evil spirits. That, however, is biblically inaccurate. When we examine demons in the scriptures, it becomes pretty clear that they create certain physical challenges that we see every day. For instance, there was the woman with a spirit of infirmity who could not stand up by herself (Luke 13:11-17). I see people like this at my church every Sunday. There was the epileptic boy or the lunatic (moonstruck or mentally ill) in Matthew 17:14-21, Mark 9:14-29, and Luke 9:37-43. There was the boy that had a mute spirit in Matthew 12:22-23. All of these are common physical conditions that we see every day. According to the scriptures, demons can cause these conditions. Now, that is not to suggest that all persons exhibiting these traits have a demon. However, please note that no reasonable person can likewise conclude that these conditions are purely natural. If we earnestly defer to the scriptures on the issue, surely, we can conclude that evil spirits cause some of them.

If we are to be honest, that means that we must surely know that these conditions don't magically disappear when we confess Jesus as our Lord. I have never seen a person healed merely by a confession of Jesus as Lord. Even if you have, you have not seen it regularly. It is definitely rare to see a physical healing result from such. So, we know that demons can create physical issues.

We also have examples of demons creating other issues. For instance, in Acts 16, Paul confronts a woman with a demon of divination (a psychic demon). My last example is that of the Gaderene demoniac in Luke 8:26-39. Here we clearly see a man that is emotionally torn. The Bible says that he spent his nights in the tombs crying and cutting himself. Therefore, we know that demons can affect people physically, mentally, emotionally, and spiritually. This is a fact. It may not be what some people want to hear, but it is true. Furthermore, if you want to experience healing, you must consider this reality. If you are unwilling to even consider this possibility, then I have to wonder how serious you are about your greatness?

I want us to take a close look at the life of the Gaderene

demonic. Here is a guy that has a life riddled with conflict like Naaman. He cannot get along with the people (Luke 8:29). He lives with the dead and visits with the living (Luke 8:27). Again, he is crying and hurting himself. If we take a close look at the text, we see that the first three types of conflict are present: circumstantial, relational, and internal. I think it is fair to say that he has a lot of conflict in his life.

The difference between the inner conflict of Naaman and the inner conflict of this man is rooted in the source of the conflict. The source of Naaman's inner conflict was his own heart. That means that he battled with terrible thoughts generated from himself. We see this as the text reveals his thoughts regarding how he thinks Elisha should minister to him. The Gadarene demoniac, however, has an inner conflict in which he is battling evil spirits—spirits that are trying to take over his life. Unlike Naaman, the thoughts he is fighting are not his own. He is battling the thoughts of something else. I can imagine him saying to himself, "I am going into town," when something else says, "No! You are going to the tombs." I can again imagine him saying to himself, "I am going to hang out with some cool people." I can then imagine something else saying, "Those people don't like you. You should knock them out. All they ever do is try to lock you up all the time. Don't put up with it." There is clearly another inner voice that he cannot control.

That is the primary key to knowing that something is wrong. 2 Timothy 1:7 says that "God did not give us a spirit of fear but of love, power, and a sound mind." The Greek word for sound mind in the passage means *self-control*. That means that God has given us the ability to control our thoughts, which in turns empowers us to control our behavior. In fact, one of the fruits (evidences) of the Holy Spirit's leadership in a person's life is self-control (See Gal. 5:22). Again, that means that God's Spirit gives us the ability to control our self. It is pretty clear that even God Himself does not want to control us. He wants us to be in control and thereby responsible for our behavior. What this all means is this, if you have an area of your life that you are not able to control, then something else is likely in control of that area.

It is clear from the story of the Gadarene demoniac that he had little control over his emotions and his behavior. It is the first sign that there is a possible demonic presence. You should not have inner thoughts and desires that you cannot control. If you cannot stop thinking about it, no matter how much you try; if you cannot help the urge to do something wicked regardless of your best efforts, chances are you have a demon. It is not the kind of thing we like to talk about, but it is a reality. Furthermore, our unwillingness to talk about the truth of this matter is what I suspect contributes to the vast amount of immoral behavior in the Church.

I will never forget how God made demons and demonic thoughts real to me. In the early years of my salvation, I began to experience what is called "sleep paralysis." For those of you unfamiliar with this term, it is when something comes upon you at night, and you suddenly cannot breathe or move. It is a very helpless and frightening situation. It is one that a lot of people experience worldwide. Just Google "sleep paralysis" and you will get an endless list of links regarding the subject.

These experiences began to happen just as God was endowing me with the gift of discerning of spirits. So not only did I see and hear spiritual things, I also felt spiritual things. Knowing that I was ignorant and afraid of what was happening, Satan seized on the opportunity. Likewise, I began to experience sleep paralysis many times a month. This experience lasted for what seemed like a whole year. It was horrible! Yet, in the midst of it, I learned about the power of the name of Jesus. I saw with my own eyes how demons flee at that name.

On one occasion I learned something else that was very valuable. I was saved out of a Hip-Hop lifestyle. Not that anything is wrong with Christian Hip Hop, but I was not a Christian Hip Hop artist. In fact, my lyrics were very far from being Christian! During those years as a Hip-Hop artist, I tried various ways to get inspired. Initially, the methods I tried were typical. I listened to other rappers, or other forms of music to inspire me. At some point, I started running dry on inspiration, so I listened to dark music. That worked for a while, but soon I was struggling to be inspired again. Next, I resorted to listening to angry songs, drudging up bitter memories, and sitting in the dark. Eventually, that worked so well that it became my normal process. All I had to do was follow this deviant process and wait for inspiration. Not long after creating the right atmosphere, I heard the first line of the song. They always appeared as audible thoughts. From there I tuned to a flow that poured out of me like water. Little did I know that an evil spirit was providing me with those thoughts. I was sort of suspicious that something was wrong because the content of the songs were very dark in nature. In fact, my friends refused to listen to them because they said that the lyrics painted scary images in their minds.

Well, after my conversion and all of that was behind me, I had a strange encounter with this evil spirit. There I was in my room, now saved. At the time I had not written a song in a year or two. Then suddenly I heard these very poetic words in my mind. The composure of the words was so great that I decided to lie on the my and listen to them. However, as I was listening to what I thought were my thoughts, I realized that I was thinking something else at the same time. I was thinking, "Wow! That's dope." Then it suddenly occurred to me, "If I'm thinking, "Wow! That's dope. Then who is that rapping?" Suddenly, something pinned me to the bed. Next, I heard a hideous voice burst out in laughter. I was terrified, but I had been through this sort of thing before. That being the case, I knew to call on Jesus. Once I did, the experience ended as quickly as it began.

Nonetheless, what I took from the experience was priceless. I learned that it is possible to have two separate and distinct thought patterns playing out in the mind. One of them is sure to be yours. The other will belong to either God or a demon. For instance, when they belong to God, you may have a struggle in the conscience. Paul said in Romans 9:1, "I know that I am not lying *my conscience bearing me witness.*" That means that he recognized that he was going in the right direction. He was confident in this fact because he had no thoughts from the Holy Spirit challenging his chosen path. Sometimes, however, those other thoughts belong to Satan's crew. When he is the originator of the thoughts you receive, they will be oppressive, tempting, and ungodly in nature. Let me say that the use of the word "ungodly" does not refer to evil. Ungodly thoughts can be thoughts to do good things for the wrong reason. Regardless of who speaks, one thing remains true—you will not be in control of those thoughts or voices.

We can see a perfect example of this principle in Daniel 2:29. In the previous verses, King Nebuchadnezzar had a dream and had searched for someone to interpret it. After a while, it came to his attention that Daniel could interpret the dream. There was a catch, however; not only did Daniel have to explain the dream but he also had to tell the king what he dreamed. When we catch up to Daniel and the king in verse 29, Daniel said, "Oh king, as you lay on your bed, thoughts came into your mind and the Ancient of Days is revealing to you things that will happen in the future."

Get the picture; the king has "thoughts" that "came" to his mind. It is clear from the description that these thoughts are not the king's thoughts. The phrase "came into your mind" also indicates that these thoughts were not under the king's control. We soon discover why he had no power over these thoughts. It was because, as Daniel said, the Ancient of Days (God) was showing the king the future. See, those thoughts that are not under your control are not yours!

Likewise, the Gadarene demoniac had an inner struggle with something that he could not control. That something (demon) was keeping him from experiencing God's best for his life. Just like Naaman, something on the inside was working against the dream on the outside.

Let me say that this is not a book on deliverance. Therefore, I will not go into detail about how to resolve the issue. For more information on demons and deliverance, see books by John Eckhart, Derek Prince, Kimberly Daniels, and Frank Hammond.

(For those of you that are interested in more teaching about demons and deliverance, I have free teachings on my YouTube channel. Those teachings are more detailed than this section and contain instructions for casting them out.)

Initially, I was not going to deal with the subject of demons in this book. The Holy Spirit, however, would not allow me to ignore the issue. Since this part of the book deals with internal conflict, it is only right that I cover the subject with balance. To really get to that place of restoration in your life, some of you will need to confront the issues of your heart, like Naaman—issues such as lust, pride, insecurity, bitterness, fear, unforgiveness, and meanness. Others of you will find it necessary to confront the demons in your life. Yet, for some of you confronting a combination of both will be required. Regardless of the situation, just know that dealing with internal conflicts are the starting place for getting the thing that is hindering your greatness out of your way. Addressing the issues of the heart is a sure way to get a hold of that dream.

Seeing the Inner Conflict

Naaman said, "I said to myself…" He was hearing that little inner voice speaking to him. Sometimes that little voice likes to talk in pictures. We call them imaginations, daydreams, and night dreams. The Bible calls them dreams and visions.

Naaman clearly saw a healing scenario in his mind. The same thing happens to us all. Whether it is demonic, divine, or our inner voice, conflict has a way of speaking to us visually. My dreams are the best way to get a grip on my inner conflicts. Now, I know that this too is a taboo subject in the Church. Some churches are afraid of dreams. Actually, they are not afraid of dreams, but what they think might result from following a dream. Some people fear that a dream will lead us away from Christ. To be fair, that is a possibility. For that reason, I always advocate learning how to discern the source of dreams. It is not that hard.

Over the years, I have come to understand a few things about dreams. In a future book, I am going to write extensively about the subject. But for now, I will briefly discuss the matter.

Ecclesiastics 5:3 says that a dream comes through much activity. In other words, a busy, hectic, or stressful day might find its way into your dreams. For that reason, people consider dreams to be worthless. However, since this book is about using conflict to your advantage, dreaming is essential. Getting to a healthy place means that you must not ignore the issues you see in your life. Sometimes we do not see our problems with our physical eyes. Sometimes we see them as they are revealed to our spiritual eyes in dreams.

Here is an example. In the 1990s I broke off a relationship with a woman I was dating. I did so because I had given my life to following Jesus Christ and because she was a painful burden to my heart. So, I had to let her go. A few years later I started to have a reoccurring dream. It was a dream of me physically assaulting this woman. Every dream was not identical, but the theme was always the same. It was always about causing her physical harm. Now, I am not one who abuses women, so these dreams were extremely troubling to me. After seeking God about the issue, He revealed to me that I had not grieved the relationship. He also showed me that I was harboring anger in my heart towards her. So, when given the opportunity I released it to Him. After doing so, I never had a dream of that nature again.

I had an inner conflict of which I was unaware. The reason I had no awareness of that conflict was due to the removal of the stimulant (the woman). Remember, inner conflicts arise from circumstantial or relational conflicts, which are both external. Since I did not have something to stir up these hidden issues, I thought I was okay. Many of you are in the same predicament. You have anger, bitterness, unforgiveness, insecurities, and more hiding in your heart and you think you are ok. But if God were to bring the person's face or the memory of that event into your mind, you would find those old feelings stirring up on the inside. In my case, they showed up as visual images. Just imagine what would have happened if I had not dealt with the issue revealed by the dream. Imagine me taking this kind of baggage into my marriage.

A few chapters back I wrote about how my wife's return to the workforce stirred up my inner issues. The external problem was inflaming the internal issue. I also wrote about how God used dreams to reveal those issues to me. I have many such examples I could share, but for the sake of brevity, I will not share another. Nonetheless, know that your inner dream life is vital to your ability to understand how to move forward; for that reason, I always journal my dreams. I journal the God dreams, the demonic dreams, and my dreams. I do so because it allows me to see things about myself that I might not see during the day, due to my busy lifestyle. I recommend that you do the same.

Divine Ideological Conflict

The last type of conflict I see in Naaman's story is ideological conflict. This type of conflict occurs when there is a clashing of ideas and doctrines. More precisely, this type of conflict is visible when our thoughts conflict with God's views and ways. God, speaking through Isaiah, says in chapter 55:8, "My thoughts are not your thoughts. Neither are My ways your ways." In other words, God is telling us that the likeliness of us disagreeing with His ideas are great.

Naaman's story bears out this reality. God told him to do something that conflicted with what he imagined as a possible solution. The result of these crashing ideas was a stalemate. Naaman did what so many of us do in these types of situations. He walked away from the potential to step into a greater chapter of his life. What great opportunities are you about to forfeit?

One of the most memorable videos I have ever watched was a debate between an Evangelical and Charismatic theologian. They debated the relevancy of the supernatural spiritual gifts in 1 Corinthians 12. It was awesome to watch the conflicts unfold and the division it created. It was fascinating to know that the divide was rooted in ideological differences. Both had sufficient training. Both understood the Greek words in the passages. Both articulated their points of view clearly. Yet, they could not reach the same conclusion. Moreover, that was ok. We have the right to disagree with others based on our various points of view. I believe ideological conflict is at the heart of most problems. It is, in fact, the reason there are factions in every major religion. However, what happens when the opposing idea comes from God? How do you argue with the Person described as "the Word" made flesh? The word "word" in the passage is the Greek word "Logos;" It means; the embodied idea. Jesus was the very essence of God's thoughts and ideas. Everything He did revealed what God thought about every situation? We discover that He had thoughts of compassion when He healed the sick and raised the widow's dead son to life. We saw what He thought about propaganda in the Church when He turned over the tables and whipped the offenders until they left the building. We read in amazement as He revealed the merciful thoughts of God to a woman caught in the act of adultery. Jesus was a revelation of God's mind and His heart towards humanity.

Some people have probably never considered that God is a thinking being. We often think of being made in the image of God physically. We negate the fact that our ability to think and create, love and be angered, to forgive and chastise, are qualities that we share with our Creator. Moreover, just as we are thinking creatures, so is God. Jeremiah 29:11 says, "I know the thoughts I think towards you…" Again, Isaiah

55:8 says, "My thoughts are not your thoughts..." Folks, God thinks! This statement tells us that He has ideas. He, in fact, had an idea for how to resolve Naaman's situation and He has one for yours too. The question is this; whose idea will you embrace? Will it be your idea? Sure, it is terrific that Naaman saw a way to fix the problem. I applaud the fact that he at least thought about finding a solution. There is something admirable about someone who actively pursues change. Again, it revealed his audacity to dream. Still, if he knew what to do, why was the blemish still on his greatness? Why had the problem not been resolved, if he had the solution? What about you? If you know what to do, why are you still struggling with the same thing? Maybe God's ideas work better, though they are different from ours.

In July of 2018, my wife and I attended a marriage retreat. We had not participated in one in over ten years. I know that sounds awful, but we had our reasons for not attending. First, God blessed us with children every two years. Eventually, we had four of them. Likewise, finding childcare for four kids for three days was no small feat. Last, we had a disdain for the teaching at the retreats we attended in the past. Everyone seemed like a record stuck on repeat. Every year it was the same thing, "Husbands love your wives" and "Wives respect your husbands." It was not the monotony that got on our nerves, but the lack of insight into the scriptures that addressed the subject. As you can see from my writings, I am one who enjoys insightful expositions of a text. I cannot stand to hear a speaker get up, recite a passage, and then merely transpose what he or she read. I like to listen to messages composed after a thorough investigation of the text. That was not happening at the marriage conferences we attended.

However, this time was different. This time, we heard from a couple that spent many years teaching and studying marriage. They were a breath of fresh air. What made them unique was the fact that they spoke on the same subject, "husbands love your wives, wives respect your husbands," but they did so in a meaningful way. They did not merely recite the text. They explored the idea of respect and love in the context of marriage. As they did, they presented research, statistics, and many real-life illustrations to support their conclusion. At last, my wife and I were satisfied. Satisfaction, however, had its price. Little did we know that God would use that time of instruction to uncover our faulty thinking. We understood that God uses people to speak into the lives of His people. Still, we did not expect the presenters' message to affect us like it did. At the end of the last session, the impact of their teaching had me near tears. I was near tears because I realized that I had a problem with honesty. No! I am not implying that I am a habitual liar. However, I admit that there were times when I hid information from my wife to protect her from something, I thought would unnerve her. A few times over the years, various financial situations blindsided us. Most of the time, it was due to my dishonesty about the status of our finances. Their teaching made me realize the gravity of this behavior and its potential to keep my marriage from maximizing its greatness.

I was not the only one affected that day. My wife also saw herself in a way that broke her heart. Her revelation upset her so much that she too was near tears. Like me, she also thought her reasoning justified her behavior. What was happening to us? Why did this happen? It occurred because our thoughts clashed with God's thoughts. We encountered ideological conflict. Likewise, there were options on the table. God had revealed His hand. We were at liberty to keep playing our hand, or take the one He freely offered to us. We all have the same choice. Once God confronts us with His idea for getting us to reach greatness, we must decide. Do we keep our idea, or embrace His? It is kind of reminiscent of the idea of "this water or that water over there."

Naaman had the same choice before him. He could either force the issue, insisting that Elisha do it his way. Alternatively, he could take the idea the man of God received from God and apply it to his life. His initial response tells us that he believed his idea was better. It says he chose to turn and walk away. Turning away meant that Naaman eventually turned his back to the man of God. It was an intentional insult. Are you insulting God? Are you choosing your way? What about your greatness? By turning his back on God's idea Naaman was deciding to turn his back on his greatness. What about you?

Why We Argue with God's Thoughts

I think that answering the question regarding why we argue with God is essential to address. This story aids us in understanding this dilemma. Let me start by saying that there are two primary causes that undergird this problem. They are both found in Elisha's instructions to Naaman: "Wash and be clean." I know, it seems odd that such a statement contains the answer to our problem. However, it does.

The first reason that defines why we argue with God's thoughts is that He challenges who we are. He tells us that we can be more than what we are; go further than where we've been; and dig deeper to mine out our best. He tells us we are great. The simple truth of the matter is God wants more for us than we want for ourselves.

God wanted more for Naaman. How so, you ask? Just think about the statement, "Wash and be clean." God was saying, "My child, you don't have to be dirty anymore. You can be clean. You can be whole. You can be great and reach your full potential." God was communicating to Naaman that there was a better version of himself waiting on the other side of his obedience. All he had to do to experience it was to accept God's idea for his future. It seems like a simple idea to embrace. Yet, he is not alone in struggling to receive God's goodness. Many people struggle to accept God's ideas for their life and circumstances because they find it hard to believe that there is a better version available to show the world. Many quit their marriages because they don't think it can live again. More than a few men stop trying to be fathers for fear of failure. Some careers never begin because someone dared not believe they could fulfill its requirements. Yes, we struggle to believe life can be better, but only because we will not let go of our ideas.

I will never forget meeting one of the most beautiful and shapely women I had ever met in person. She was so attractive that her beauty was hard for any man to ignore. In fact, sexual harassment was unfortunately commonplace in her life. Yet, as stunning as she was, and with all the attention in the world, she still struggled to embrace her beauty. She could not see what we saw. She even struggled with wanting to change her appearance. It was fascinating to me. How could someone so beautiful struggle to see what the world clearly affirmed as beauty? It all confirms that seeing the good in us can be a struggle even when it is evident to others.

Some of you are great artists and performers. Others are great speakers and teachers. More than a few of you are highly intelligent. Though many of you fall into these categories, you still struggle to explore who you are in Christ. You fear that you are not enough, though God clearly says you are. Don't fight God's idea. Like Naaman, you are everything that He says and more. Nonetheless, you will only know that truth by letting go of your idea and embracing God's.

The second reason that explains why we argue with God is found in the same command, "Wash and be clean." The same words that told Naaman he could be more are the same ones that tell him he has not arrived. The command reminds Naaman that he is dirty. Isn't facing our shortcomings the hardest thing to do? That's what this book is all about. It is about confronting the parts of yourself that keep you from exhibiting the best parts of you. Encountering God is exciting. He tells us that we can be great, but He also requires us to grow into that place. Likewise, growth involves exposure.

In fact, it is the nature of God's word to expose who we are. His word is called a lamp unto our feet and a light unto our path (Psm. 119:105). The key words being "lamp" and "light." In other words, God's ideas give us the ability to see. That is both good and bad news. It is good news because it allows us to see who we are and where we are in life. It is bad news because it shows us who we are and how far we have yet to go.

I love the book of Genesis. It is the book of firsts. I find it interesting that one of the first things that God teaches us about Himself is that He speaks. Then He shows us the power in His mouth. With His words alone, He called forth the earth's beauty. His words exposed lush vegetation, beautiful animals, and magnificent sea creatures. Still, the same voice that called forth beauty also called forth the creeping things. The same voice that revealed the lion also unveiled the serpent. The same ideas that showed us the butterflies also unmasked the spiders. We love it when God's thoughts show us the good in us. We, however, are not always quick to embrace the creeping things that blemish our greatness.

God told Naaman that he could be more. God is saying the same to you. His word challenges us to be more, to go beyond our limitations and live in His idea for our life. However, God's word also exposes error in us.

I hate that we have a generation of believers that disengage from God's perceived unlikeable nature. Today, some preachers oblige the idea that God's goodness is affirmed by His good deeds. Some go as far as completely disavowing the Old Testament because of the depiction of God's hostile acts; acts deemed as unloving and cruel. However, the truth is God does not always make us happy. Sometimes His words provoke us deep within. They make us ponder where we are in life.

Again, think about what God is saying when He says, "Wash and be clean." He is, in essence, causing Naaman to confront his condition. By inviting him to be clean, He is also calling him to face his wretchedness. That is what happened to my wife and me at the marriage retreat. We heard God's thoughts, and they clashed with our own. Suddenly, the lights were on, and we realized that we had not arrived at perfection. God's thoughts called forth the creeping things in our marriage. He was exposing us to greatness while telling us we were not there yet. He was encouraging us to reach for the goal.

Very few people like confrontation. We don't want to

talk about our faults and sins. We don't like to listen to our critics. We don't like bad reviews after we take the risk of exposing our works to the world. We hate it when people tell us we are not enough. However, what was viewed, as "not enough" was an invitation to experience more! What if Naaman had rejected the idea that God was saying that he was not enough and embraced the notion that He was saying, "You are more than what you believe?"

Getting to the place of seeing God's best in the ideological conflicts means acknowledging the good in what looks like the worst. The same is true of the other categories of conflict. In this chapter, we explored four different types of conflict. None of which are designed for our destruction, instead each is there to help us construct and uncover the greatness in us.

As I close out this chapter, I want you to remember that there are four categories of conflict: circumstantial, relational, internal, and ideological. Learn them well and learn to harness the power of these conflicts. Learn to use them to your advantage. If you do, you will see that God is trying to show you something. For some of you, conflict will reveal an upgrade to your character. For others, these conflicts will expose flaws that threaten your greatness.

Reflection Activity:

- Write out the various types of conflicts in your life. Is it a circumstantial conflict, a relational conflict, an internal, or an ideological conflict?

- Is there an internal conflict that you cannot seem to control? Try to determine if you need natural or spiritual counseling to resolve the issue. If you decide that the internal problem is a spiritual one, just know that self-deliverance is possible. It can be as simple as commanding the evil spirit to leave you in Jesus name. That being said, there are other times when you will need to seek the help of an experienced deliverance minister.

- Ask God to open your eyes to see what your dreams may reveal about your heart. Consider the way you feel in the dream, any themes, or challenges the dream presents to you.

- Ask yourself this question: Is there a divine idea in my head that seems to be at odds with me? If you answer, yes, then write the idea down.

- Consider whether the idea requires you to make a leap of faith? Is God asking you to grow into something bigger? For example, is God asking you to call your ex-wife to do something for her she asked for during the marriage? Is God asking you to provide your boss with a list of proposed completion dates for your projects? Is God asking you to take your racially biased co-worker out for lunch? *(This is a great time to revisit the idea of the pros and cons of obedience.)*

Chapter 9

The Keys to Restoration

Naaman went on an amazing journey. He traveled all the way from his country to a foreign nation to be healed—a nation he previously raided. In his journey, he encountered conflict that threatened to suck the life out of his dream of healing. However, thanks to excellent counsel, a willingness to confront the issues of his heart, and his ability to get past the circumstantial, relational, internal, and ideological conflict, he was restored. The question I want to answer in this chapter is, how; How did Naaman get restored? The answer to this question should help you see restoration in your marriage, friendships, career, your reputation, your nation, and if possible even your health. Naaman's example teaches us how to be restored!

Acceptance

One sure way to shortchange yourself from receiving God's dream for your life is to deny the reality of what He places before your eyes. The first thing I established in this book is that you are great. That is a truth that you must come to accept. Likewise, you must also realize that your greatness can be blemished. Then I told you that sometimes the tension in our life leads to tearing in our life. That tearing results in a revelation of something hiding in our heart. Dealing with the revelation of what is revealed gets a bit tricky. It gets tricky because often the personal issues revealed by conflicts are painful to face. For some of us conflict shows us that we still have childhood issues controlling our life. For others, we may discover that we feel inadequate in some way.

I will never forget the first time I noticed growth in my life since becoming a Christian. The reason it was so memorable to me was that I had an issue I thought I would never get past. Like so many of us, I experienced some things as a child that made me angry. In my mind, a release of anger was a way to resolve a conflict. In fact, violence was often my very first thought. It was such a problem that I was actually afraid of being angry because I was not sure I could control myself. Therefore, I opted for avoiding conflicts. Then one day, as I was taking a friend home, I found myself at the center of a car accident. The person in the other car ran the stop sign and crashed right into the front end of my car. I was immediately afraid. Not for me, but for the other guy. I was not confident that I could control my anger if he created problems. I was so used to anger showing up to defend me that I did not know another way to respond.

When the other driver and I got out of our cars, something unexpected happened. I spoke in a calm voice and said to him, "Don't worry man. Accidents happen." Then I smiled, and all was well. That was until the police officer showed up to write up an accident report. He wanted to know who caused the accident. The other driver immediately pointed to me. Suddenly, anger began to arise in my heart. But it was not at all what I was used to experiencing. It was a gentle anger. I might even say it was more disgust than anger. It did not include over the top uncontrolled expressions, or thoughts about how to cause physical harm. In that moment of conflict I realized that God upgraded my character. That incident revealed a new person to me. Soon I was back to smiling, but not about the situation. I was smiling because of the revelation of God's' change in my life; I was excited about my growth.

There were other times in my life, however, where God used conflict to reveal my shortcomings. On one occasion, God showed me my pettiness.

My wife and I grew up differently. I grew up in a house with a father that cleaned incessantly. He washed the walls, the light switches, and everything else. Cleaning was and still is something that he enjoys. Likewise, he heavily insisted that things be kept neat and orderly. That meant that my brothers and I learned to be careful and attentive to how we did things. The affect of growing up under such conditions meant that we never spilled things. My wife, however, grew up in a more liberal setting. As such, she was more careless in her conduct. If she spilled something, it was no big deal. In her mind, she thought, "If you spill something just clean it up and go on with your life."

I remember her spilling water on the carpet on one occasion. This, however, was not the first time. It seemingly happened every other day. When she spilled the water on this particular occasion, I got angry. Noticing the look in my eyes, she made haste to clean up the mess. From her actions, she seemed apologetic. I also noticed something odd. I noticed that I was affecting her freedom and hindering her ability to freely be herself. At that moment, I had a flashback to my childhood, and how anxiety filled we became when we spilled something on the floor. Then I started to notice that my wife was feeling the same.

At that point, I had a choice to make. I could continue to be angry and start an argument—about water! I mean, after all, she did spill something, frequently. I could have easily made this all about her faults. Or, I could take this moment of conflict and use it to examine myself. I chose the latter.

Choosing to let my self see myself was the best gift to my marriage. But, I had to make a choice to look at my role in the conflict. I had to use the finger I was using to point at her, to point at me. In fact, my willingness to yield to what God was doing in my life helped to develop a servant spirit in me. Instead of fussing about spills, I learned to serve her. I also learned what it means to cover her.

Here is a personal example that occurred the day after I wrote this chapter entry. I am adding it because of how it clearly depicts the reality that our inner issues can affect our destiny. Furthermore, it describes how conflict brings the source issue to the surface.

It all took place after I arrived home from a Bible class. I walked in the door, and suddenly I was confronted with an angry letter from my neighbor. Not only did it contain infuriating content, but a stinky attitude. She made sure to write the date in the proper text: "September 14, 2017". It was formatted differently from the body of the letter, which she wrote in "ALL CAPS." It was clear that she wanted my wife and me to know that she was angry.

Why was she so angry? Well, a couple of months before all of this I purchased a new van for my wife. It was supposed to replace one of our three cars, but I never got rid of mine. Now, I know that this sounds bad. However, I did try to donate my car, but I lost the title. In my mind, getting a replacement title was another daunting MVA task, so I procrastinated. Now I had four vehicles in front of my house. Plus, this meant that we parked the fourth vehicle in a not so neighborly way from time to time. Needless to say, the letter was warranted and her anger was justified.

As one might expect, upon reading the letter my wife and I were a bit livid. Now the question was, how was I going to respond? "Was it true," I asked myself? "Yes, it was," I concluded. At that moment I was faced with a decision. Hear me when I tell you that I did not want to make the right one! Here was a conflict right in my face. Was I going to take it personally that her method of delivery was off-putting? Or, was I going to take this as a moment to do some self-reflection. I chose the latter.

As I reflected on the situation, I came to understand the problem. The tone of this letter was a sign of something that had been brewing in her heart. She is a very orderly person. Her grass is always cut. She and her husband are always outside ensuring that the trees are trimmed, and the flowerbed is kept. Then she looks over to my yard and sees the opposite. You see, I was indeed a lousy neighbor, not just to her. I was a bad neighbor to all of my neighbors. She was just bold enough to say what I am sure the others wanted to say.

Upon more inner reflection, I concluded that I was a dream chaser who neglected his responsibilities. At the heart of it all was procrastination. That was a significant revelation. Why? Knowing that I procrastinate around things I do not like to do is as much of a threat to my ultimate dream, as pride was to Naaman getting restored. I had to consider that there is not one successful procrastinator. Anyone that obtained his or her dream did so through diligence. They also had to learn how to teach themselves to complete all tasks, those they liked and those they didn't.

I hope these stories are helping you to see how this all works together for your good. Self-discovery is the real power in the truth of how God uses conflict. Again, Naaman discovers this as well. The circumstantial and relational conflict in his life created an opportunity for him to listen to his inner voice. After the prophet ruined the ministry moment and after Naaman saw the conflict in the circumstances he said;

> "*Indeed,* **I said to myself,** *'He will surely come out to me, and stand and call on the name of the* LORD *his God, and wave his hand over the place, and heal the leprosy.'* [12] *Are not the Abanah and the Pharpar, the rivers of Damascus, better than all the waters of Israel? Could I not wash in them and be clean?*"

Look at what his heart revealed. Naaman had already figured out a plan for his restoration. And when his plan conflicted with God's plan his pride revealed itself! It only gets better as you keep reading. Not long after Naaman unveiled his plan, he came up with an alternate idea regarding the water. Likewise, he assumed that his plan was better than God's. That is interesting to me for many reasons; one, if he knew how to fix the problem, it would have been fixed before that moment. And two, God owed Naaman absolutely nothing. He was not a Jew, which meant he was not in a covenantal relationship with God. In fact, he only knew about the God of Israel because of the Israeli slave girl he took when he raided Israel. He was asking for a lot considering the circumstances. Naaman had a sense of entitlement. It was that sense of entitlement that almost cost him his dream of restoration.

This tidbit of information teaches us that the outer blemish, leprosy, though a problem, was not the real hindrance to his greatness. Leprosy did not stop him from accomplishing his goals. Leprosy did not stop him from being the king's number one man. Leprosy did not stop him from conquering kingdoms. Likewise, your blemish, your sickness, your lying, your gambling, your alcoholism, your substance abuse, your (fill in the blank), is not stopping you from moving forward. Some of you are good at functioning in a dysfunctional state. Naaman's real problem was not the immediate threat leprosy posed. Sure it threatened to steal the future from him. As I said in an earlier chapter, what is a soldier without a hand? However, I want you to consider that even though his blemish threatened his future, nothing was more threatening than the thing hiding in his heart. Leprosy did not hold him back from moving forward, but pride did!

What he had in his heart was so dangerous to his future that it almost made him throw it away. What is God revealing to you in the midst of conflict? What stumbling block is He trying to show you? What impedes the greatness of your future?

Naaman's was pride. I dare say that pride or the sense of entitlement is at the heart of why we divide things in our life that God wants to heal. How often do we look at the other person in the conflict as the source of the tension? How often do we consider that conflict is the result of "two" or more opposing forces? The real question to ask is, what is my role in the conflict? Conflict is a time to look at you!

Understanding how to use conflict to see myself has improved every area of my life. When I face circumstantial conflict, I look inward. I pay attention to what my inner voice is saying. The same is true about relational conflict and internal conflict.

Now, let me repeat something I said earlier about facing the person in our heart. Sometimes, facing the person in our heart can be very challenging. Many times people do not like to confront the person in the mirror. That is because what they see of themselves might take them back to painful places in their childhood. My recommendation for severe issues is counseling. I know that in some Christian circles "counseling" is a dirty word. However, the truth is that counseling is designed to help you healthily process your feelings and experiences. Notice, I said that counselors help you to process your feeling in a "healthy" way. I tell people all the time; your feelings are processed one way or another. Some people will process them at the bar. Some will process them in the bed of many lovers. Some will process them through violence. Others will process them in other unhealthy ways. The bottom line is that we all process our feelings one way or another, good or bad. That being said, if God provides a method and a place for you to process them healthily, then you should take advantage of that service.

Here is some Bible on the subject. James 5:16 says, "Confess your faults one to another that you might be healed." For the record, I know that James is speaking of sin. However the principle in the passage indicates that some things only get healed when we talk to someone about the problem. Again, I encourage you to let someone help you process the deep problems that surface during a moment of conflict. Allow someone to assist you to see that negative thing that God is revealing. Give yourself the gift of life! See a counselor.

If you do not know where to find one, you should start by asking your pastor. You can also call your insurance company. One of them can point you in the right direction.

Perspective

The second thing that you need to consider as you seek to obtain restoration in your life is perspective. We have dealt with the subject of perspective in an earlier chapter. I cannot stress to you enough how important perspective is in this process. If you are going to grow in this process, then you need to know how to view the problem correctly.

In my example of my over the top response to my wife's carelessness, I made a choice. That choice was the beginning of the rest of my life. And it started when I decided to see the situation correctly. First, I had to realize that a happy marriage was the goal (vision), not clean carpets. The other option was anger, unrest, and stress. I had my choice of waters before me. So having the right perspective of the goal was crucial. Then I had to choose to see my part in the conflict. Again, I could have blamed my attitude on her carelessness. Or, I could see this as an opportunity to demonstrate my love for her and help her clean up the mess. What I saw as the goal, governed my choice of action. Still, I had to see the situation correctly.

Likewise, you must have a goal in mind. Naaman's goal was restoration. What is your goal? Is it to have a more prosperous marriage? Is it to have financial stability? Is it to have better health? Is it to be a better parent? What is your goal and how do you see it?

Then you must choose how you see the conflict. Naaman saw it as an obstacle that deterred his forward movement. His servants, however, saw it as an opportunity to be restored. How do you see the conflicts in your life? Are they a chance to get even with the offender? Are they convenient moments to complain about the circumstances? Or, are they doorways to a time of self-evaluation and growth? What is your perspective of the conflicts in your life?

Repentance

Well, the subject of repentance is never an easy subject to tackle. This is especially true today in our culture of "Don't judge me" and "We don't need to repent. We're already forgiven." In my opinion, the problem is not that we do not like to repent. The problem is that we do not really understand what it means.

Most people define it as a 180-degree life-turn in the opposite direction. For example, that means that we go from lying to telling the truth, or from fornication to celibacy. Some define it as saying you are sorry for a sinful act. Let me say upfront, I agree with both of these definitions. The Hebrew word for repent, *nacham* definitely means to be sorry. So we know that feeling a sense of remorse for our actions is a component of repentance. However, when we look at the Greek word, *metanoeo* we see a different meaning. Repent in the Greek means to think differently or afterward reconsider. In other words, it boils down to a change of mind. This distinction is essential to make. "Why," you may ask? Well, for starters this book is about understanding that the person we see on the outside is often different from the person on the inside. Remember our earlier examples of David and his brothers. David was frail on the outside and brave on the inside. His brothers were strong on the outside but weak on the inside. This tells us that it is easy to change our behavior to suit our environment.

Have you ever visited with a church that worships differently than your home church? I have. I have also found that it is easy to conform to the standards of an environment when it is convenient.

For example, my home church is an African American Full Gospel Baptist Church. In our services it is common to see people yelling high praises to God, dancing in the aisles, running around the front, bowed down in worship at the altar and more. This is our church culture. Sometimes, however, I visit with more conservative churches, and it is incredible how hard it can be to be your self in someone else's culture. Often, I find myself struggling in that environment to be free with my expression of praise. On the inside, I am boiling over with praise, yet on the outside, I am barely making any noise. What is my point? The point is this; sometimes people teach us how to act. We know how to play the role of a husband or wife. We know how to play the role of a man or woman of God. We know how to be what we need to be when we need to be something else. But often our thinking is still the same. Jesus said it this way in Matthew 15:8, "These people honor Me with their lips, but their hearts are far from Me." In other words, they look good on the outside, but inwardly they are rotten.

A Change in Direction

The truth is, genuine repentance is not just an outward action. It is an inward action as well. Now, it is true, that a change of mind will lead to a change in your behavior. This is what Naaman experienced as well. In fact, he underwent two outer changes. He had a change of mind that resulted in a change in his behavior. That change of behavior was reflected in a change in his direction. He also had a change in his perspective regarding how He saw God.

First, there was his change in behavior that resulted in a change in his direction. This is the part we love to preach about, the moment when he obeyed the man of God and bathed in the dirty waters of the Jordan River. But, there is more to see in the passage than his action of bathing. There was a direction change. 2 Kings 5: 14a reads:

> **14** *So* **he went down and dipped** *seven times in the Jordan, according to the saying of the man of God;*

Look at the bolded part of the passage. It says that he went "down." Then read 2 Kings 5:9 and pay attention to the bolded part of that passage.

> **9** *Then Naaman went with his horses and chariot, and* **he stood** *at the door of Elisha's house.*

It tells us that Naaman "stood" at the door in his initial meeting with Elisha. Do you see it yet? Do you see the contrast in Naaman standing and dipping down? The pride in his heart made him stand. But the humility he received after appropriately responding to conflict allowed him to come down from his high-mindedness. Dipping was a sign of humility. In fact, when you read the instructions from Elisha, you find that he said absolutely nothing about dipping. His instructions were to "wash and be clean." The direction change was a sign of the change in his mind.

It was the change in his thought process that ultimately led to the change in his life. He started his journey with a passion for apprehending his dream. He also came with his own way to solve his problem. He even had a self-conceived vision and expectation of how he should be treated. Yet, he left with a new understanding. In the end, his attitude was different towards Elisha.

A New Theological View

Not only did Naaman have a change of mind and attitude towards Elisha, but he also had a change of mind regarding God. When he arrived, he was a follower of the Syrian god, Rimmon. When he left, he was a follower of Jehovah God of Israel.

Verse 15 shows us his attitude change. It read's:

> **15** *And he returned to the man of God, he and all his aides, and came and stood before him; and he said, "Indeed, now I know that there is no God in all the earth, except in Israel;*

Verses 17-18 show us his inner change. They read:

> **17** *So Naaman said, "Then, if not, please let your servant be given two mule-loads of earth; for your servant will no longer offer either burnt offering or sacrifice to other gods, but to the* LORD*.* **18** *Yet in this thing may the* LORD *pardon your servant: when my master goes into the temple of Rimmon to worship there, and he leans on my hand, and I bow down in the temple of Rimmon—when I bow down in the temple of Rimmon, may the* LORD *please pardon your servant in this thing."*

There is something interesting happening in this verse that brings us full circle to what I have been saying. In this passage, we can clearly see that Naaman is willing to do something externally contrary to his internal desire. He says though he may worship Rimmon with his body, he will never again do so with his heart. Some of us operate in an opposite manner. We worship on the outside while setting our heart on other things. That is why understanding how to respond to conflict appropriately is so necessary. It helps us see who we really are. Ultimately, we see a repentant Naaman. Likewise, that simple act enabled him to achieve his dream. He changed his mind and changed his life! You should do the same.

Support

As I mentioned earlier, one thing I love about this story is the fact that Naaman had so many people in his corner. How many people today, can say that they have such a strong community of support like Naaman? He had the support of his slave girl, his wife, his king (boss), the man of God, and God Himself. Everyone was rooting for him to win. There were two particular types of support systems in Naaman's life that I want to address: One, someone to inspire him, and two, someone to keep him accountable to his dream.

The Inspirer

It was terrific that Naaman had so many people in his life that wanted him to win, but ultimately the dream was set in motion by the willingness of a slave girl to share some good news. It was her declaration to her master's wife that God could fix his problem that made the difference. One of the biggest keys to getting what God has for you is your ability to hear about God? We all need inspiration. In addition, we need people who are willing to speak in a way that makes us know that we can accomplish our dreams.

God made this concept real to me one day after work. I was walking out of the building pondering issues about healing ministry when I asked Him a question. I said, "Lord, how do we get people into a mindset to want healing?" He said, "Preach to them! Tell them about My ability to heal. That will open them up for healing." Romans 10:14

immediately came to mind, "How shall they hear without a preacher?" It became clear to me at that moment that telling someone that their situation can be different is the key to getting faith to stir in their heart. That is what happened to Naaman. He heard someone say that his situation could change.

To inspire us God may choose to allow us to encounter one of two proclamation methods: a preached word, such as the word that came through the slave girl. To preach means to "tell." Her example is a modest variation of preaching. The other way in which God may choose to inspire us is through a testimony. A testimony is a reciting of things that we have witnessed. It is valuable because it is a "test-of-money" or a test of the value of something. When someone goes to court, the testimony offered is considered valuable to the outcome of the case. The same is true today. A good testimony lends credibility to why we should believe something.

The Apostle Paul's preaching is an excellent example of the power of a testimony. Paul never preached a complicated narrative regarding salvation. He merely told his testimony of what he "saw" and "heard" when He encountered Jesus on the Damascus Road. His testimony was so valuable that by sharing it, he changed the world around him. His testimony also raised the faith level of those to whom he spoke. In fact, it had such an impact on them that they responded to the Gospel favorably. A good testimony inspires people to believe that all things are possible with God.

The Account-holder

The other person we all need in our life if we are to move toward our dream effectively is an account-holder. The account-holder is the person in our life that we allow to challenge us. For some of us, it is our spouse. For others, it is a friend or a mentor. Whoever it is, we all need someone to help us stay the course.

Not long into the process of writing this book I lost my focus. I was not distracted by sin or family problems but by my past literary works. I had written and published my first two books. They were selling pretty well and received phenomenal reviews. They were both regarded as the best books ever written on the subject of hearing the voice of God by those who read them. Then I read a review that pointed out some grammatical errors in one of the books. The reviewer still gave it a great five-star review, but it alarmed me to read about the errors. From that moment on I obsessed about going back through both of my books correcting the errors. The problem was that I did it so often that I neglected writing this book.

Having witnessed all of this, my wife said, "Stop re-editing the books! Chalk it up to growth. You had to start somewhere, and you did. You worked with what you had. The next book will be professionally edited, and you will have a record of your growth." Then she said, "Do you see music artists going back redoing their early works, even though the quality of the new work is better? They don't go back and redo all of their music. And that allows us to see how far they came." The last thing she said hit me like a ton of bricks and put my soul at rest. She said, "You know, the time that you are spending chasing down errors is the time you could invest in the new book. Every time you look back you are losing your focus."

What she said was right. So I left it alone and started writing this one. At that moment God made her my account-holder. She helped me to stay focused.

I think this is a great time to deal with the irritation that often results from the account-holders in our life. Naaman was challenged to think differently. While we see no adverse response from him regarding his servants' counsel, we can speculate that he might have felt a bit agitated. Just imagine being a great leader whose servants challenged your direction. No one likes to be challenged. I certainly don't! However, please note that there is a difference between encouraging and antagonizing. Naaman's servants encouraged him. It is so important to know the difference. Knowing the difference allows you to accept good counsel. That being said, an account-holder will get on your nerves! But that is okay. Just know that their motivation is not to ruffle your feathers. Their goal is to get you across the goal line. Getting started is good. Still, someone has to be there to ensure you finish—that person is the account-holder.

The other reason it is so important to have "the inspirer" and the "account-holder" in our life is because we often become discouraged on the journey. In my previous example, you can see that I was getting discouraged. Likewise, Naaman became discouraged. He traveled a long way then was insulted, neglected, and given a word he didn't like. In our journey towards the thing God wants for us, each of us will encounter opposition. Opposition always leads to some form of discouragement. I don't care how strong of a person you are; know that opposition threatens the faith of us all. That is why it is important to have a good support system in your life. Naaman had a "starter" word to get him going and a "pusher" word to get him to the finish line. That is what each of us needs in our life. Someone willing to tell us that things in our life can be better; and, someone who will push us towards the finish line when things get hard.

There is another important thing to consider regarding having an "inspirer" and an "account-holder" in our life. The person(s) that hold these positions should be intimately involved in our life. It is imperative that we understand the power of relationship if we are to see restoration in our life.

I said it earlier, but it bears repeating: The slave girl and the servants are people who knew Naaman. Likewise, it was out of that relationship that they were able to have an impact on his decision. The only person who was not able to affect his decision was the one person he did not know, namely Elisha. This truth communicates to us that the people who wield the most power in our lives are those with access to it.

Something else to take note of is the value of these relationships. While the word of the Lord had a hard time finding its place in Naaman's heart, the servants with him knew how to get him to listen. They said, "If the man of God had asked you to do some great thing, you would have done it." Their statement is a clear indication of their intimate knowledge of him. It was out of that knowledge that they spoke to him.

Divine Strategy

In the section above I mentioned how a good support system includes those who inspire us to start and finish our journey. But what is the value of a word from a person if we do not also get a word from God? In part, we see that God spoke to Naaman through the circumstances. There is, however, a more evident word from God in the mouth of the prophet Elisha. Likewise, we all need an Elisha experience. I know that in today's church culture people are doubtful that God speaks directly to us. That being the case, we have come to depend on the Bible as the sole source of divine communication. And I agree that we should give it its due reverence. Others, in conjunction with the Bible, use other indirect methods of communication with God. These include signs and or special circumstances called "doors of opportunity." Nevertheless, the biblical model established for us, in both the Old and New Testaments, is one of both indirect and direct communication from God.

That means that we should be a people that can hear from God via the scriptures. We should also, however, be able to hear from him directly. Why? Well, because the Bible teaches us that God likes to give precise information. Never will you see a place in the scriptures where God is unclear about His instructions. In every place where there was a question, such as Daniel's regarding his visions: the prisoners in jail with Joseph regarding their dreams: Ezekiel or John regarding their complex revelations, you will see that God provided a crystal-clear answer. Never once did He lead people into a fog. Some might say, "Well, what about Abraham? God told him to go to a place He would later show Him." Though this is true, I would have you to consider that God only left the destination a mystery. His instructions regarding the journey, however, were precise. God speaks with precision!

It was the precision of God's instructions that led to Naaman's restoration. Sure, he had his own solution to the problem. He was a real leader and as such was driven to solve problems. This problem, however, was one that he could not reason away. Therefore, he needed a precise set of instructions for how to resolve this issue in his life. You need the same.

This means that you need to learn how to hear God's voice. There are many great books on the market that address the issue. I recommend my two books, *God, Is that You, Me, or the Devil? How to confidently know God's voice.* This particular book is described as a manual on the subject. In it, I cover every conceivable aspect of the matter. Its big focus is on knowing the difference between God's voice, Satan's voice, and your voice. My other book, *You Can Hear the Voice of God Clearly; How to go from the still small voice to the voice of God*, deals with how to hear God's voice clearly. This book will explain to you what hinders your hearing and how to resolve the problem. Either book is an excellent resource on the subject of hearing God's voice.

Let me end this chapter with a review of the keys to getting restored. Getting from the verse 1 of our life, where we have an issue, to verse 14, when we are restored is rooted in these five keys: **1.) Acceptance:** A willingness to embrace the revelation of the thing that is revealed, via conflict, that keeps us from being all that we can. **2.) Perspective:** A willingness to see the situation correctly. **3.) Repentance:** A willingness to repent; to change how we think. **4.) Support:** A good support system that includes, someone who is willing to see God's ability to change our circumstances and someone who will challenge us to stay the course until we obtain restoration. **5.) Divine Strategy:** And last, a word from God that provides a strategy for success.

Ensuring that these five keys are in our life will open the door to the next level.

(There are two other keys, consistency and resolve. Both are discussed in the Undefiled Greatness Journaling Workbook)

Reflection Activity:

- Take a moment and review this chapter. Thoughtfully consider the five keys to restoration. Consider what you need to do to see them at work in your life.

- Journal your thoughts about each.

- Are there any discrepancies between your thoughts and your behavior? If so, identify them and work towards genuine repentance .

- Identify any new perspectives that you notice developing about your situation.

- Identify the "inspirer" and the "account-holders" in your life.

- Pray and ask God for a strategic word. Be sure to write it down. Remember, the word from God may ask you to do something uncomfortable.

Chapter 10

The Power of Restoration

Restoration represented a dream for Naaman. It was his dream to rid himself of the thing that threatened his greatness. Likewise, restoration represents your desire to be all that God has designed you to be in every area of your life. For Naaman, it was the healing of his body. For you, it might be the healing of your marriage, your family, your career, your mind, your ministry, etc. Restoration is something that we all need at some point in our life, and Naaman shows us how to get it.

When reading the passage about Naaman's life, it is so easy to become fixated on the healing of his body. But when we take a closer look at his life, God shows us that a lot more than Naaman's body was healed.

God Restored Naaman

Verse 14 is so exciting. It reads:

> **14** *So he went down and dipped seven times in the Jordan, according to the saying of the man of God;* **and his flesh was restored** *like the flesh of a little child, and he was clean.*

Naaman endured a lot to obtain his dream of healing. Now, it was his. After traveling a great distance, causing anxiety in the heart of the king of Israel, being insulted by the prophet, counseled by his servants, and receiving a strange prophetic word, he was finally healed. At last, he was rid of that outer facing issue that threatened to rob him of his future. He was restored! Isn't that what we all want—to see our hard work and aggravation pay off? Naaman's paid off big time.

One thing I need to talk about is the reward of responding appropriately to conflict. Naaman's story teaches us that there is indeed a reward.

At first glance, it seemed that God simply gave Naaman new flesh. That is until you realize that God gave him so much more. In fact, verse 14 says that God gave Naaman flesh like that of a little child. What does that mean? It means that God did not give a 50-year-old man, 50-year-old flesh. God did not merely restore him to where he was before. Neither did He simply replace what Naaman lost. Instead, God went the second mile and gave Naaman more than he expected. God made it worth the effort. That is a real marvel considering that Naaman had an attitude problem. Also, let's not forget that this is the same man whose nation raided Israel earlier. It is not only a sign of God's goodness but His mercy.

This is good news for us. It all means that God is not merely trying to get us to the goal line. He is actually trying to take us far beyond it! Still, doing so means responding appropriately to the conflicts in our life. Remember, it is the conflicts that reveal the issues that stand between us and our dream.

A New Perspective

So far, we have looked at perspective in general terms and in relationship to repentance. Now I want to address the issue of perspective concerning the subject of restoration. Here is something else about perspective to consider. Not only did God heal Naaman's flesh. He also repaired his perspective. Before God healed Naaman, he held to the point of view that Jehovah God was of lesser power than the Syrian god, Rimmon. But after his encounter with the true and living God, who made his dream a reality, Rimmon was suddenly of lesser value to Naaman. God was now magnified in Naaman's life. Can you imagine depending on something for years that was never able to produce anything substantial in your life? Then one day you cross paths with something that actually worked to resolve your issue. I am sure that Naaman prayed to Rimmon for his healing. It is pretty clear in the story that he wanted this blemish off of his greatness. That, my friends, is the power of restoration. Restoration has the ability to cause us to see God in a glorified way.

We see another potential benefit as we consider the reality that Naaman's perspective regarding the water was probably improved. One can only assume that the dirty waters of the Jordan were suddenly not so bad after all. In fact, I imagine that it later served as a memorial of a great place in his life. Just imagine what he might have said to himself and others every time he passed by that water.

That is one of the many things that I love about God. No one can repurpose a thing like Him. Just think about the things in your life that you thought you had to have. Think about how you can look back now and say, "Thank God I did not marry her," or "Thank God I did not buy that house," or "Thank God I did not…" See, God has a way of changing our perspective regarding the dirty waters in our life. Suddenly, the bad things become a good reminder of His mercy. Again, it only happens after Naaman was restored. There are just some things you cannot appreciate until you have gotten your reward. A great man of God once said, "You have never had a steak so good until you have eaten it in front of those who did not want you to have it." In other words, some things are only enjoyed after you have been through something. Naaman's life indeed teaches us that we can see things clearer afterward.

God Restored Everything Naaman Touched

Naaman's life also teaches us something else. It teaches us that resolving our issues, resolves how those issues affect the lives of those around us. Isn't it wonderful to think that my healing is healing for everyone else in my life as well? You may be saying, "How so?"

Well, remember, I revealed in an earlier chapter the broad impact of Naaman's issue on others. I showed you that it was the leprosy that was at the heart of the discussion between his wife and servant girl. It was leprosy that was at the center of the reason why he met with the king. It was leprosy that almost brought the two kings to war. It was leprosy that made the king of Israel distressed. It was leprosy that landed him an audience with the man of God. It was leprosy that was at the heart of his conflict with the man of God. Finally, it was leprosy that was the cause of the conflict in verse one between "who" he was, and "what" he did! So, the disease was at the heart of the personal issue, the domestic issue, the national issue, the international issue, and the church issue. And guess what? When God restored Naaman's flesh, he also removed the thing that was at the heart of the problems in everyone's life. Likewise, when God removes the issue in your life, then everyone around you is impacted.

Let me use this example; once the drug addiction is gone, so is everyone else's drama. There is no more crying over stolen money. There is no more wondering if the person will make it home safely. The multiple arrests go away. The marriage can now move forward. The children can now move forward. The city has one less criminal on its streets. The taxpayers have one less person to support. The world has one less person missing from its care. Yes, restoration is a powerful thing!

For me, getting rid of the neglectful behavior in my life allowed others in the community to be at peace. It gave a visual representation of responsibility to my children. It gave my wife peace knowing that it was not stressing the neighbors. It brought value to the houses in the neighborhood. It made a great impression on those who see me with a Bible. And the change in my life was possible because of a moment of conflict that revealed the issue behind my issue. We all know that the use of the drug or any vice is not the issue for addicts, whether gamblers, smokers, porn or sex addicts, etc. The habit itself is always rooted in something in the heart. It could be anger, or bitterness, or just pain. Whatever it is, conflict will draw it out. From there, it is a matter of choosing to move in the direction of healing and not separation.

As you can see, restoration is a powerful thing. Obtaining restoration in your life means restoration for someone else too!

Reflection Activity:

- Take a moment and think about how better your life would be if you were healed of your issue.

- Take some time to consider how your issue may have impacted the lives of those around you. Now think about how their lives might be improved if you allowed God to heal you of that issue.

- Earlier in the book, you made a list of people and things affected by your issue. Using your imagination, I want you to see how your restoration positively affects the people and things you listed. Write down what you see.

This activity gives you a stronger sense of connectivity. Upon completion you will see how the resolution of your problem positively impacts the world. You matter more than you know!

Chapter 11

He Tore You, To Restore You

One of the reasons I wrote this book was to cause growth in the Body of Christ. Part of growing up into Him that is the head, namely Christ, is learning how to manage conflict. As I have stated before, Paul, Peter, James, John, and Jesus emphasized the desire that God wants us to be of one mind. They also heavily stressed how we should respond to conflict in our life. Therefore, it is important to God that we achieve the unity of the faith. Likewise, doing so means that we work at resolving conflicts.

I have been around the Church for a long time. I have seen marriages fall apart in less than a year. I have even seen them fall apart after many years. I have seen friends separate. I have seen churches split. I have watched the body of Christ viciously attack other parts of the body. I have seen a lot in my few years on earth. That being said, one thing stands true in every single situation; an inappropriate response to conflict is sure to destroy what God is trying to build.

Our inability or unwillingness to respond appropriately to conflict stems from the reality that we do not recognize that God is trying to help us not hurt us. Romans 8:28 says, "All things (good and bad) work together for the good of those that love God and are the called according to His purpose." Also, the other thing we fail to realize is that God is not surprised by what happens in our life. We must know that God's allowance of a situation in our life means that there is a purpose for it. I like to share with my followers that understanding the truth of Romans 8:28 means acknowledging that the bad things in our life are merely good things in disguise.

We also fail to comprehend the vastness of His love for us. That is why He gave me "He tore you to restore you" as the underlying premise for this book. It is true that God tears us to restore us. Just think about it. The Bible says that He opened Adam up and took one of his ribs (Gen. 2:21-22). He tore him! It also says that He made Adam a wife from that same wound. God took something out of him to make him better equipped to fulfill his destiny. He tore him, to restore him. Likewise, God allowed a conflict in Naaman's life that exposed something that was a threat to his greatness. And by dealing with that issue, he was restored.

Naaman was Desperate

Here is the last thing I want to point out about Naaman as I close out my thoughts on this issue, he was willing to dip seven times to get his miracle, he was desperate. What do I mean? Well, most preachers focus on the obvious idea of the text. They see that Naaman was restored because he was tenacious and obedient. This perspective is built on the idea that the strategic word of God called for Naaman to wash seven times. This meant one of two things: Either the miracle was progressive, and each wash improved his condition. Or, he would not see the miracle until the last wash. Either way, the manifestation of the miracle was validated by the seventh dip. This assessment of the text regarding tenacity and obedience is accurate. There is undoubtedly a benefit to being tenacious and obedient when trying to receive something from God.

What I want to point out, however, is his desperation. Remember, he endured a lot to get to this miracle moment. The fact that he was willing to wash seven times tells us how desperate he was to get it. It revealed the passion of his heart.

Imagine this; see him finally choosing to obey the prophet. As he applies the strategic word from God, he washes to get clean, and nothing happens. So, he washes again. Still, nothing happens. Then a third, a fourth, a fifth, and sixth time, and still nothing happens. Then he washes one last time and is healed.

I want you to imagine him each time he dips to wash. See him feverishly dipping and each time doing so more passionately. See him fishing for that miracle and saying to himself each time, "Come on, come on, you have to work, you have to work. Please work!" Do you see how desperate he his? This man wanted a change in his life really bad. Now consider the fact that he was about to throw it all away over a conflict about which water was the best environment for a miracle. Also, please note that our level of disappointment is always equal to our level of opportunity. Big disappointments come from missing out on significant opportunities.

Can you imagine how disappointed he would have been in the morning? Can you see him thinking to himself later when his body started hurting, and more of his flesh was falling away, "Man! Maybe I did over react about the water." Can you see yourself after the divorce saying, "Man! Maybe I did over react..." Or, after your church has split saying, "Man! Maybe I did over react to..." You see, the truth is that Naaman's dips reveal how badly he wanted this blemish off of his greatness.

Likewise, I know that many reading this want the blemish out of the way of your greatness; whether personal, or in your plutonic relationships, or in your marital relationship, we all want that thing that is keeping it from being great out of the way. Just consider that no one gets married to get divorce later. No one works for the same company for 20 years to part ways on bad terms. No one pastors a church wishing to fight with the congregants. No one wants to throw away a friendship they spent years building. Now, I realize that we must let some things go. But generally, we are desperate to see these special things in our life blossom. We want a great marriage. We want great friendships. We want great work situations. We want great (fill in the blank). But the question is how desperate are you? Are you desperate enough to take the challenge of looking at your role in the conflict? Are you desperate enough to harness the power of conflict for personal change? Are you desperate?

Let me say this as I conclude this book: From this point forward, you must choose your path. Some people have suffered considerable stress in their marriages. Others in their relationships with their co-workers, others like me, with neighbors, yet more than a few churches are steeped in conflict. Nonetheless, here is the reality; you can choose to continue pointing your finger at others; an act that guarantees division and destruction in your family, church, career, or friendships. Or, you can choose to use the moments of conflict in your life to see what God is revealing to you about you. If you choose the latter, I promise you that God will heal you and everything that your issue has negatively impacted abroad. Remember this, the only reason He tore you, was to restore you! Likewise, I want you to remember that restoring you means restoring everything in your life, that includes those things affected by your issue.

Bringing it Full Circle

I started this book with the assertion that we are what we think. My basis for this was Proverbs 23:7, "As a man thinks in his heart, so is he." Some believe that this verse warns us against becoming victims of our thinking. My argument, however, is that the sum product of our person is revealed by our thinking. Likewise, coming to that conclusion is import-ant to our growth. Ultimately, God desires to change us into the image of Christ. However, doing so means confronting the thoughts that define who we are. Last, confronting who we are means allowing conflict to reveal both our strengths and our weaknesses. It also means giving God permission to repair our broken areas. Ultimately, courageously facing the man in the mirror leads to our growth.

Bonus Chapter

A Word from the Lord

A Word to Ministers

When thinking about conflict, it is hard to ignore the conflicts in the pulpit. Therefore, it is prudent for me to write a word of wisdom to the men and women of God. Today, we have the most egregious things happening from our pulpits. We have rumors of men raping and molesting young boys and girls. We have financially irresponsible behavior. We have raging homosexuality. We have alcoholics and substance abusers. We even have prophets who herald prophecies that fail and then blame it on the people. Also, it is general knowledge that we have big morality problems. And these are just some of the issues.

How are these things possible? Well, I believe it is because of our lack of accountability to the Body of Christ to which we are called to serve. Somehow, it has gotten into the spirits of those who wear the cloth that we answer only to God. Such thinking causes some of us to think that we are invincible. Unfortunately, it has led to the behavior that I described. It is the same type of mentality that I point out in the life of Elisha. Remember, it was how he mishandled the ministry opportunity with Naaman that led to the conflict. Likewise, there are conflicts in the Church, and I dare to say that at the helm of it are those of us who wear the cloth. Some are conflicts between people, some are conflicts in theology, yet others are conflicts in morality.

One passage of scripture that preachers like to hide behind is 1 Chronicles 16:22, "Touch not my anointed and do my prophets no harm. This passage is what we enjoy quoting to those beneath us when we go wayward. Somehow, we suppose that we alone are of value to God. Then we go on hurting the Body of Christ as if those in the pews have no significance to the Lord.

I want to challenge you, however, to see the Body of Christ as something precious in the sight of God. Oddly enough, that value I ask you to see is present in the same passage of scripture that we use to exalt and create our untouchable status.

You see, 1 Chronicles 16 is not esteeming the place of the servant of God. It is establishing the value of the nation of Israel. It is vital that we see this truth precisely so that we do not make the mistake of "touching the Lord's anointed thereby causing them harm!"

The biggest problem with this passage is that it has been misinterpreted and misapplied. So, let's look at the verse closely. When the chapter opens, David has just placed the Ark of God into the temple. In a moment of exuberant joy, he pens the words that are also found in the book of Psalm. In his writing, he takes the time to recall Israel's journey from Egyptian bondage to freedom in the Promised Land (Canaan). In doing so, he establishes for us that the subject of the passage is the nation of Israel. That is made clear to us in verse 17, where it says, "... to Israel for an everlasting covenant." David then goes into a few details regarding that covenant: One detail being Israel's allotment of land in Canaan (verse 18). Then David writes about their travels, at which time he mentions that one of the other benefits of the covenant was God's divine protection. Verses 20-21 communicate that to us. In these verses, David clearly states that He (speaking of God) allowed no one to harm them (speaking of Israel). Then comes our favorite verse to quote as a protection of the servant of God. As you read, however, I want you to keep the audience in mind. Verse 22 says, "Touch not My anointed, (speaking of Israel) and do my prophets, no harm.

So, what is the point? The point is this, the Body of Christ is the anointed that is not to be touched! Clearly, this means that this passage does not only apply to the servants of the Lord. It also refers to how God wants us to see the value He has for the Body of Christ as a whole. It also has further implications for those of us of the cloth. Here is something that we should consider. If God has threatened that no harm should come to His people, then we too should recognize their value to Him when we stand and walk before them.

Acknowledging this truth also means that we must regard our opportunities to minister before His people as divine appointments from God. Therefore, we must care just as much about how we do our job, as we do when it comes to getting it done.

Sometimes Ministry is Inconvenient

When my oldest child was born, it was one of the scariest times of my life. There I was with this tiny 5 pounds 6 ounce little bundle in my arms. She was helpless and innocent. She was also dependent on me to take care of her. However, I must admit, my wife and I were scared; being first-time parents and not knowing what to do with this little life, we were a bit jittery.

In the midst of our jitters, we found a great pediatrician for our daughter. The thing that stood out about this woman was her availability. At my daughter's first visit the doctor concluded the visit by handing us a sheet of paper with two phone numbers on it. One was the office number, and the other was the emergency contact number. The emergency contact number was a direct line to the doctor during her off hours. It was clear from the document that the second number was for severe or life-threatening emergencies only. But as new parents, a life-threatening emergency was anything. So, as you may have guessed, we used the emergency number frequently. What amazed us, however, is that no matter how many non-emergency voice messages we left the doctor during her off hours, she always called us back to meet our needs. We knew right then that this was the doctor for us. Needless to say, she has been our pediatrician for all four of our children. Likewise, it was her availability that made us so loyal. Eventually, we settled into our new role as parents and used the emergency number as it was purposed.

The point of my story is that sometimes ministry opportunities show up outside of Sunday service and Tuesday Bible study. Somewhere along the way, the call to ministry became the call to preach at churches. Likewise, preachers spend a lot of time waiting for God to give them opportunities to preach. Somehow, they lack the ability to see the opportunities in front of them daily. What I appreciate about Elisha's example is how he made himself available to Naaman's need.

The Bible says that Naaman came with all his horses and chariots to the door of Elisha's house (2 Kings 5:9). This ministry opportunity presented itself outside of normal hours. The house represents a place of comfort. It is where he went at the end of the day, having spent all day serving.

I imagine that he might have had his feet up relaxing, eating something delicious, and cooling off with a cold beverage. The fact that he made himself available to serve speaks volumes about his commitment to the call of God upon his life. If we are honest, we do not want to be ready to minister in and out of season. We just want to share our gifts when invited to speak in a traditional setting. However, being prepared for service at anytime is always the call of God.

In January of 2017, God said something challenging to me. Every first 40 days of the year I give to God in a fast. I usually only drink water or fruit-based juices, and I eat nuts and grains. Also, I do so with some ease because God honors it by empowering me with grace. This particular year, however, fasting was more challenging than ever before. I found myself sneaking foods, experiencing unbearable hunger, and just not wanting to complete the fast. I knew that this meant God did not want me to fast this year. Though He did not support my fast He still had something to share with me. So, He started teaching me what He wanted me to know. At the end of the teaching moment, it became clear to me that He wanted me to fast from myself. He told me that He wanted me to serve Him by serving people. That meant making myself available to serve the needs of people no matter where I go. It meant healing the sick, without having to do a healing service. It meant ministering the word to a person in the grocery store. It meant answering questions and decluttering people's minds via answering emails and instant messages. It also meant taking advantage of the live video features on social media. It meant that I was to allow the Naaman's of life to meet with me even when I was in my comfort zone. In short, it meant allowing others to inconvenience me.

Here is something you should know; God is raising up a generation of preachers who are social media savvy. They are not a generation that is satisfied to preach only when they can get paid, or when they can be seen by many people, or by invitation. They are a generation of people who are taking Jesus' words literally. They are going into the highways and byways, the street corners, the grocery stores, and any place where there are breathing people. They are healing the sick, sharing the Gospel, casting out demons, and if possible, raising the dead. They don't like being in the house. The walls that some of us view as protection from the world are walls of restriction to them.

However, they too will need to understand that how you do the job is just as important to God as getting the job done. So, my word to the men and women of God is that they handle God's people with care. Touch, not His anointed. Treat them with care knowing that He cares deeply for them.

A Word to the Nation

In early 2015, during the United States presidential elections, God spoke to me about a season of conflict that was to come. He said to me, "I have appointed Donald Trump. I have raised him up, and he shall be pepper in the throat of this nation. I am going to bring to light those hidden things woven into the fabric of this nation." That word has been correct. Not long after, Donald Trump pulled off one of the biggest upsets in the history of the U.S. presidential elections. It was unexpected, but it was in God's plan.

Now, the fact that God said that Mr. Trump would be pepper in the throat of this nation does not make him a bad person. The point is that God was going to use him to shake things up in this country. Since he took office, we have seen the exposure of the resurgence of the Klu Klux Klan (KKK). We have witnessed wealthy influential heavyweights brought down by past sexual conduct. We have seen the exposure of the divide in the Body of Christ. We have seen the disclosure of corrupt political practices. God has been tearing the United States open, and she has coughed up some terrible things. Those things are blemishes on her greatness. They are a challenge to who she is destined to be. For that reason, God tore her so that he could restore her.

There is, however, one issue that remains to be an problem. For whatever reason, my country has decided that it should only serve its own interest. We call it "Nationalism." Howbeit, it is self-centeredness. Let me tell you something.

Nothing threatens the greatness of a country like selfishness. God told Israel that it is He that gives her power to get wealth. God wanted them to understand that any economic achievement was due to His involvement. I dare say that the same principle applies to the U.S. It is God that has given us the power to get wealth. It is He and He alone that have raised us up. Likewise, it is He that can bring it all down. I sense a warning from heaven. An admonishing that says, "You can't consume My blessing on yourself. I blessed you to be a blessing to the world. I and I alone have raised you up as a mighty well of life; to feed those who are less fortunate; to cover those who would be bullied. It is I that makes you prosper in war. And I am making you strong again."

A Word for the Church

There is one thing that stands out to me about Naaman's story. That one thing is the desperation of one man to have a body that is whole. Naaman understood that wholeness was a benefit not only to himself but, to the army as a whole. What we see is the concept of a "whole" body unfolding on two levels. There was Naaman's body and the body of soldiers that made up the army.

God is saying to tell His people that He is bringing them into a season of restoration. That restoration is going to happen on two levels. First, it will happen on the individual level. He is going to heal us as individuals and release the greatness He has put on the inside of us. He is going to blow again in this season and cause us to live. He says, "Consider the dry bones in Ezekiel's vision. Was I asking whether or not it was possible for the bones to live? No! I was asking if they could live again. And that is what I am going to do for My people. I am going to breathe on them the second wind and cause them to live again. Indeed, the world is wondering if the dry bones of My people can really live. Watch Me. See if I will not breathe again on the slain. See if I will not heal them and cause even the vilest among them to live. Ministries you thought were over will live again. Marriages that you thought were over will live again. Churches that closed their doors will reopen. I am going to cause them to be healed, and they shall live again," says the Lord.

"Secondly, you will see the importance of healing. I am healing individuals so that I can heal My Bride. You don't know or seem to understand the value of the whole. But in this season, I am going to cause you to see that you are a part of a bigger army; a bigger picture! Naaman understood that his healing meant the strengthening of his army. And I am going to cause My people to see that the strengthening of one person strengthens the Body.

Get ready! I am doing something that will bring marvel into the hearts of those that witness it. Watch and see!" Says the Lord of Hosts.

One Last Thing

I would hate to assume that everyone reading this is a Christian. If you are not a believer in Jesus Christ and struggle to understand the concepts of this book, you should know that this is completely normal. The Bible says that unless you are born again you cannot see or understand the things of God.

John 3:3

Jesus replied, "Very truly I tell you, no one can see the kingdom of God unless they are born again."

It also says that in order to have the born again experience that one who comes to God must first believe that He is and that He is a rewarder of those who diligently seek Him.

Heb. 11:6

And without faith it is impossible to please God, because anyone who comes to him must believe that he exists and that he rewards those who earnestly seek him.

Your first step toward a brand new life is your acknowledgement of the reality and existence of God. He promises that if you do He will reward you for seeking Him.

Your next step is to confess with your mouth and believe in your heart that Jesus Christ died on the cross for your sins so that you could enter into a glorious relationship with a welcoming God, who has been waiting for you.

Romans 10:9

If you confess with your mouth that Jesus is Lord and believe in your heart that God raised him from the dead, you will be saved.

Then you need to repent, which simply means to go the other way. Let go of the lifestyle of wickedness and turn towards righteousness. I hear you saying but how?

Acts 3:19

Repent, then, and turn to God, so that your sins may be wiped out, that times of refreshing may come from the Lord,

This is the great part. You do not have to walk the path of righteousness in your own strength. When you accept Jesus Christ as your Lord and Savior He gives you the Helper, the Holy Spirit. And He will do the job of inspiring in you the very nature of righteousness.

John 15:26

When the Helper comes, whom I will send to you from the

Father, that is the Spirit of truth who proceeds from the Father,
He will testify about Me, and you will testify also, because you
have been with Me from the beginning.

For God imputes or transfers to us His righteousness when we give Him our confessions of nakedness. His Spirit will fill you and empower you to live this life we call Christianity. God made him who had no sin to be sin for us, so that in him we might become the righteousness of God.

2 Corinthians 5:21

God made him who had no sin to be sin for us, so that in him we might become the righteousness of God.

Yes it is that simple. Just say Lord I know I have been wrong and I repent (I am sorry) for the life that I lived. Say Lord, I give you my weakness and my sins and I accept your forgiveness and your righteousness. Confess with your mouth, Lord I believe that Jesus Christ your only begotten Son died on the cross for my sins and was resurrected for me. Then ask Him to fill you with His Spirit and go on with your life living empowered to do right.

This next step is optional, but it is really good for you. Often, in biblical times, when a person gave their life to the Lord, deliverance was done. Deliverance is the process of casting out evil spirits that attach themselves to people. Yes, this happens. The good news is that with salvation comes healing (mental, emotional, and physical) and deliverance. If you want to go all the way follow these next simple steps.

Statement of Renunciation

Say, Devil, I renounce your presence and your hold on my life. I am now a believer in Jesus Christ and my life is now His. That means that you have no more rights to my life and I command every unclean spirit to leave me right now. Leave my emotions. Leave my mind. And leave my body. I command all illness related to your presence in my life to go with you, in Jesus name. Amen!

If you do not have a church home, then you will need to find one quickly. The Bible tells us that we should be a part of a family of like-minded people who can strengthen, encourage us, and help us to grow in the things of God.

Colossians 3:16

Let the word of Christ richly dwell within you, with all wisdom teaching and admonishing one another with psalms and hymns and spiritual songs, singing with thankfulness in your hearts to God.

If you made it to the end of the process, I would like to welcome you to the family. Now, if you read this information again, I promise you it will make more sense. The kingdom of God is not a kingdom that allows one to window shop.

One Last Thing

You must to come inside to understand it for the Bible says, "TASTE AND SEE that the Lord is Good" (Psalm 34:8). You don't get to see until you first taste!

About the Author

Kevin has been walking with the Lord for 30 plus years. His passion is teaching believers how to achieve intimacy with God; live a purpose-filled life, walk in God's power, and how to successfully and victoriously wage spiritual warfare. He is a gifted prophetic teacher and preacher, demonstrating profound biblical insight. Most notably, many consider him a balanced source of revelation and admire his commitment to connecting deep spiritual truths to the Scriptures accurately.

He is also the author of five other books titled, *God, Is that You, Me, or the Devil*, *You Can Hear the Voice of God Clearly*, *Is God Still Speaking?*, and *God-Talk: The Language of Dreams and Visions*, *God-Talk: My Dreams and Visions Journal*.

Currently, Kevin shares God's word through his online ministry. He can be heard on YouTube and Facebook sharing what God is saying and doing in the world in this hour. He also shares his heart through blogging.

By trade he is a visual artist with the Federal Government. In this capacity he serves as a lead graphic designer and illustrator. His hobbies include making music, creating art, martial arts, and enjoying his family.

He resides in Maryland with Tanya, his wife of 19 years. Together they have four beautiful children, Autumn, Caleb, Aaron, and Noelle. He is also a long-time member of the First Baptist Church of Glenarden where he and his wife lead the Newlyweds In Discipleship ministry and serve under the leadership of Pastor John K. Jenkins, Sr.

Ministry Resources

To hear or read Kevin's teachings
visit one of the sites below.

www.facebook.com/kevinewintersministries

kevinewintersministries.youtube

Reach out to Kevin

kevinewintersministries@gmail.com

Undefiled Greatness *Journaling Workbook*
Harnessing the Power of Conflict to Maximize our Greatest Value

This is the perfect companion to the main book. This book allows you to jot down your thoughts feelings and expereinces in one place so you can better analye the voice of God through the conflicts in your life.

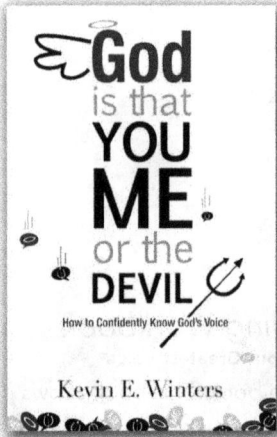

God, Is that You, Me, or the Devil?

Called a manual on the subject of hearing the voice of God, this book covers every conceivable aspect of the subject.

You Can Hear the Voice of God Clearly

"I think God is trying to tell me something." If you have ever thought that to yourself, then this is the book for you. This book teaches the believer how to hear God with clarity. It takes you from the still small voice to the clear voice of God.

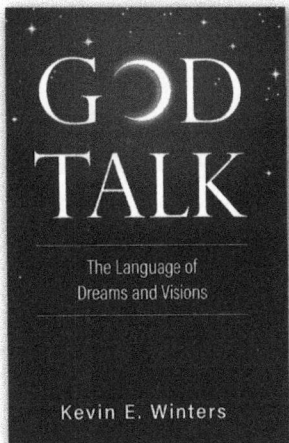

God-Talk: The Language Dreams and Visions

Job 33:14-15 reveals that God like to speak to us at night, more specifically through dreams and visions. This book talks about the range of visionary experiences and teacher the reader how to decode God's language.

God-Talk: The Language of Dreams and Visions Journal

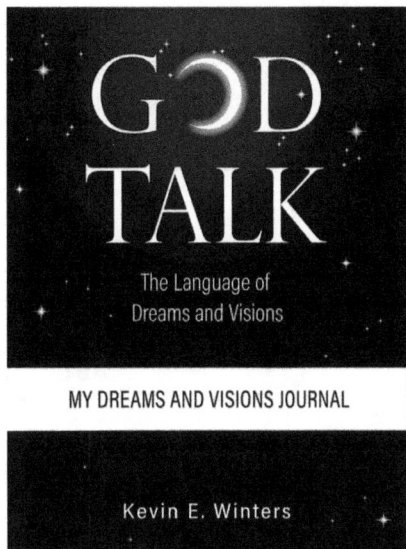

This is the perfect companion book for the God-Talk parent book. It allows you to easily record, organize, and recall your entries about your dreams and visions.